THE HAUNTED MAJOR

"HOPPED ABOUT IN A GROTESQUE AND UNDIGNIFIED ECSTASY"

THE
HAUNTED
MAJOR

BY ROBERT MARSHALL

With an Introduction by
JOHN UPDIKE

and the original illustrations by
HARRY FURNISS

THE ECCO PRESS

THE ECCO PRESS
100 West Broad Street
Hopewell, New Jersey 08525

Published simultaneously in Canada by
Publishers Group West, Inc., Toronto, Canada
Printed in the United States of America

Library of Congress Cataloging-in-Publication Data
Marshall, Robert, 1863-1910.
The haunted major / by Robert Marshall ; with an
introduction by John Updike and the original
illustrations by Harry Furniss. — 1st ed.
p.   cm.
ISBN 0-88001-669-8
I. Title.
PR6025.A67H38   1999
823'.9—dc21   98-44504
CIP

9 8 7 6 5 4 3 2 1

FIRST EDITION 1999

TO
MY MOTHER

INTRODUCTION

GOLF is a spooky game. Occult forces are clearly at work as we play. Balls vanish in unaccountable directions, glass walls arise in the direction of the hole, putts run uphill. The phenomena recorded in *The Haunted Major* all ring true, especially in relation to the hapless beginner who is our hero: "I let drive a second time, with the result that the ball took a series of trifling hops and skips like a startled hare, and deposited itself in rough ground some thirty yards off, at an angle of forty-five degrees from the line I had anxiously hoped to take." The "anxiously" is an uncharacteristic admission for Major the Honourable John William Wentworth Gore, 1st Royal Light Hussars, a sublimely self-confident snob and self-proclaimedly "the finest sportsman living." It will take all of golf's devious powers of humiliation to bring him low, and it is one of this little novel's achievements that by the end, boastful cad though he is, we are rooting for him.

Published in 1902, before the literature of golf amounted to much—before Arnold Haultain wrote *The Mystery of Golf,* before Bernard Darwin began his decades of inspired journalism, before P. G. Wodehouse launched his incomparable series of comic golf stories, before Bobby Jones elegantly committed his thoughts on the game to print—*The Haunted Major* provides a classic portrait of a hotly contested match, one hard to top in its violent swings of momentum. Haunting, interestingly, remains a theme of modern golf literature, most impressively in the apparition of the mystical teacher Shivas Irons in Michael Murphy's *Golf in the Kingdom.* And there are lesser texts involving a heavenly replay of the Hogan-Fleck playoff in the 1955 Open, or an extraterrestrial tournament matching up the revenant greats of every era against one another. None of these spooks are as vivid and vehement as the ghost of

Cardinal Smeaton, whose Scots curses ring in the dazed Major's ears while his transparent bones bedevil his eyes. In truth, we all play golf accompanied by a demon, an inner voice who taunts us and advises us and all too rarely floods us with sensations of golfing grace and power, such as the Major feels when he grips the Bishop's ancient clubs: "My legs and arms tingled as if some strong stimulant were flowing in my veins."

Cardinal Smeaton never existed, but a close approximation did exist in the person of the first Scotsman to be anointed a cardinal, David Beaton (1494–1546). Beaton, educated at the universities of St. Andrews and Glasgow, and then at Paris and Rouen, was the third son of a Fife laird and the nephew of James Beaton, archbishop of St. Andrews, whom David succeeded as archbishop and primate of Scotland in 1539. Beaton was a considerable politician, of the French-alliance persuasion. As the trusted adviser of James V he dissuaded the monarch from following the anti-papal policy of England's Henry VIII, and he helped arrange the marriage of James and the daughter of Francis I of France.

These were awkward times, however, in which to be a Scots prince of the old church: Protestantism was spreading on the Continent, and George Wishart, a grammar-school master in Montrose, caught the contagion. Accused in Scotland of heresy in 1538, Wishart fled to Europe but returned in 1544, preaching at his peril and converting John Knox, a former priest and ecclesiastical notary who became a spearhead of the Protestant movement. Beaton was a hard-line enemy of the Reformation and saw to Wishart's arrest, trial, and death by burning in 1546, in St. Andrews. To quote the Blue Guide to Scotland: "Beaton watched the burning in comfort from the castle walls. Two months later several friends of Wishart, headed by Norman Leslie, son of the Earl of Rothes, seized the castle, slew Beaton, and hung his corpse over the battlements to prove he was dead." The conspirators held out for two months, during which Beaton's body remained unburied, cast into a dungeon and covered with salt, "to await," as Knox, one of the beseiged, explained, "what exsequies his brethren the bishops would prepare for him." The *Encyclopedia Britannica* mildly relates that "although John Knox and others have exaggerated his cruelty and immorality, both were harmful to the Roman Catholic Church in Scotland, which he tried to preserve by repression rather than by reform."

My encyclopedic sources do not mention Beaton's prowess at golf, but since he had been a university student at St. Andrews, with an uncle established in the cathedral, it is not unlikely he took his whacks at a game already so popular in the fifteenth century that Parliament three times sought to ban it, on the grounds that it was distracting young men from their archery practice. So the author of *The Haunted Major* may have sound historical reasons for having his ghostly Cardinal claim, "Noo, in ma day, I was unrivalled as a gowfer; there wasna ma equal in the land. Nane o' the coortiers frae Holyrood were fit tae tee a ba' tae me." Smeaton explains his passionate interest in the Major's match by telling him that his opponent, the champion Jim Lindsay, is "a descendant in the straight line o' ane o' my maist determined foes … and ony blow that I can deal tae ane o' his kith is a solace to ma hameless and disjasket speerit." It is the *Columbia*

Encyclopedia that throws light on this particular dark spot of Scots history. Its entry for "Sir David Lindsay ... (c.1490–c.1555), Scottish poet" tells us that "As a writer he was a harsh satirist and moralist who directed most of his invective against the Roman Catholic Church. He never formally left the church, but his exposure of its abuses gives him a place second only to that of John Knox in bringing about the Scottish Reformation." The embers of these fiery old quarrels still give off some heat, and the author, in making Beaton so winning a ghost, offers an olive branch, three and a half centuries after bloody events.

Robert Marshall, the author of *The Haunted Major*, is absent from all but the most compendious reference books. He was born in Edinburgh in 1863, attended the universities at St. Andrews and at Edinburgh, and then joined the Duke of Wellington's cavalry regiment, attaining the rank of captain in 1895. He retired in 1898 to become a writer and playwright, and died in 1910, before reaching the age of fifty. That he was a Scotsman might be deduced from the ringing verve of the nearly opaque Scots accent he transcribes, from the intimacy shown with the bitter turns of historic religious struggles on Scots soil, and from his satiric creation, in "Jacky" Gore, of so fatuous and arrogant an Englishman. There is a touch of satire, too, in his sketch of the American prize, the rich widow Katherine Clavering Gunter. Her beauty, we are permitted to guess, is ground under some repair: "She is quite beautiful, especially in her photographs"; "I should have thought her face was pale but for two vivid splashes of a most exquisite carmine that glowed, or at all events dwelt, on her cheeks"; "Her wonderful complexion was more ravishing than ever in the soft lamplight ... and her luxuriant hair, dark underneath, was a mist of everchanging gold on the top." Nor do the Scots escape, as it were, scot-free: a careful explanation that they are not really dour and stingy leaves us unpersuaded. A national weakness is lightly touched upon by Kirkintulloch when he says it would dishonor his father and mother if he failed to go nightly to the public house, and anyway, "I canna sleep if I'm ower sober." Not that the Major's casual consumption of whiskeys and brandies, with a golf match hard upon him, shows any less devotion to fermented spirits.

Americans will be amazed, to the point of doubting the tale's veracity, when they calculate, as I did, that a round of eighteen holes, with one player hitting a wealth of imperfect shots, takes from eleven in the morning to one in the afternoon—a mere two hours—and that the afternoon round, beginning at two-thirty, appears, even with its dramatic and drawn-out denouement, to be over in plenty of time to revive the victor from a faint and treat him to several celebrations, a stiff brandy-and-soda, and two valedictory interviews, all before he dons dinner dress and goes a-wooing. As the Scots play it, golf is a brisk walk in natural surroundings, and not a five-hour ordeal in a hand-carved Oz. As those who have experienced golf in Scotland can attest, religious sensations are not confined to haunted Sunday matches: the skylarks, the breezy breadth of the treeless links, the blowing tan grass, the plunge and rise of the sandy fairways, and the accretion of lore attached to courses centuries old all inspire a reverent sense of being, as in the Holy Land, *at the source.*

I have played St. Andrews—called St. Magnus here—but once, beginning on a May day near dinnertime and ending in the gloaming between nine and ten o'clock; my wife walked with me, across the narrow burns and beside the patches of golden gorse, out to the hook-shaped point and then back. One hits to a number of the same enormous greens a second time, at a different pin. I felt tall and ghostly, swinging my thin-bladed rented clubs, as if my feet were treading air. This was golf as a kind of sailing voyage, with the sea a constant presence—the sea from whence once came French ships and the winds of reformation.

In St. Andrews there are three sights to see: the golf course and its solemn Victorian clubhouse; the ruins of the cathedral, by far the largest in Scotland; and the ruins of the Castle where Cardinal Beaton watched Wishart burn and was then himself slain and preserved in salt. *The Haunted Major* brings all three together in a curious amalgam of religious history, Edwardian foppery, and golfing madness, somewhat as the ruddy color of Kirkintulloch's mustache "suggested equally sunshine, salt air, and whisky." There must be, we feel, a connection between the three salient features of Scotland: the beautiful wildness of much of its landscape, the austerity of its Presbyterian brand of Protestant Christianity, and its national passion for golf. The Major is an alien amid these barbaric elements, and one of the sources of his narrative's comedy is the mellifluous innocence of his frequently startled prose; he is the prototypical colonizer blundering through the tortuous mysteries of the colonized, and the reader feels the pleasure of order restored when he at last seeks out "the best morning train from St. Magnus to London."

Harry Furniss's scratchy, suitably hectic drawings have become as wedded to this text as Gluyas Williams's illustrations are to Benchley and Tenniel's to the Alice books. Furniss comes as close to depicting the ineffable as one would wish, and the last two illustrations, of the Cardinal's headstand on the historic railway shed on St. Andrews's seventeenth hole and of his strenuous effort on the eighteen to blow a putt awry, linger in the mind's eye as emblems of the contortions that golf inflicts on its transported devotees.

—JOHN UPDIKE

CONTENTS

LIST OF ILLUSTRATIONS

THE HAUNTED MAJOR

THE HAUNTED MAJOR

I

ABOUT MYSELF

I AM a popular man and withal I am not vain.

To the people who know me I am an acquaintance of importance.

This is due to a combination of circumstances.

First of all, I am a youthful (aged thirty-five) major in that smart cavalry regiment, the 1st Royal Light Hussars, commonly called the "Chestnuts."

Secondly, I am an excellent polo player, standing practically at the top of that particular tree of sport ; and again, I am a quite unusually brilliant cricketer. That I do not play in first-class cricket is due to long service abroad with my regiment ; but now that we are at last quartered in England, I daily expect to be approached by the committee of my county eleven.

I consider myself, not before taking the opinion of my warmest friends, the best racquet player of my day in India ; and I have rarely played football (Rugby) without knowing by a strange instinct (born, I feel sure, of truth) that I was the best man on the ground.

In the hunting field I am well known as one of the hardest riders across country living ; and this statement, so far from being my own, emanates from my father's land agent, a poor relative of ours, and himself a fair performer in the saddle. As a shot, I will only refer you to my own game-book ; and if, after examining the records contained therein, you can show me an equally proficient man in that special line, well—I'll take off my hat to him.

The trophies of head, horn, and skin at Castle Goreby, our family's country seat, are sufficient guarantees of my prowess with big game in all parts of the world; and when I mention that I have been one of an Arctic Expedition, have climbed to the highest mountain peaks explored by man, voyaged for days in a balloon, dived to a wreck in the complete modern outfit of a professional diver, am as useful on a yacht as any man of my acquaintance, think nothing of scoring a hundred break at billiards, and rarely meet my match at whist, piquet, or poker, it will be admitted that I have not confined my talents, such as they are, to any one particular branch of sport.

In fact, I am " Jacky Gore," and although the War Office addresses me officially as " Major the Honourable John William Wentworth Gore, 1st Royal Light Hussars," nothing is sweeter to my ear than to hear, as I often do, a passing remark such as " There goes good old Jacky Gore, the finest sportsman living ! "

I take it for granted that the reader will accept this candour as to my performances in the spirit which inspires it, and not as a stupid form of self-conceit. I desire to be absolutely confidential and unreserved with those who peruse these pages, and a false modesty would be as misleading as it would be untrue to my nature.

For true modesty, as I conceive it, consists in an accurate valuation of one's own worth ; an estimate of one's self that is conceived, not for purposes of advertisement, but rather to foster one's own self-respect. Thus, were these pages designed only for the eyes of sportsmen, there would appear no other description of myself than the laconic intimation, " I am Jacky Gore."

That, I know, would be sufficient to arrest electrically the ears of the sporting world. But as I desire my singular story to interest the whole range of human beings, from the Psychical Research Society down to the merest schoolboy who vaguely wonders if he will ever see a ghost, I must perforce be explicit, even to the extent of expounding my personal character as well as enumerating my achievements.

First, then, I am not a snob ; I have no occasion to be one. I am the younger son of one of England's oldest earls, Lord Goresby, and my mother is the daughter of one of our newest marquises, Lord Dundrum. My friends are all of the very best, socially and otherwise. Indeed, I have established myself on a plane from which all acquaintances who have been financially unfortunate, or have otherwise become socially undesirable, must inevitably drop. For I hold that true friends are those whose position, affluence, and affection for one may be of material assistance in the race towards the goal of one's personal ambition.

If there is one thing that jars on me more than another, it is when a person of lower social status than my own presumes to associate with me in a style and with a manner that imply equality. I can readily, and I believe gracefully, meet people of higher rank than mine on their own platform, but the converse is, at least to me, odious.

Lest, from these candid statements, the reader might be inclined to consider me a trifle exclusive, I will frankly own that I often shoot, fish, or yacht with those *nouveaux riches* whose lacquer of gold so ineffectually conceals the real underlying metal. Still, a breadth of view of life, which has always been one of my characteristics, inspires me with the hope that the association of such people with one of my own type may in the process of time tend to the refining of the class from which they spring. Besides, one need not know people all one's life.

A keen eye for the artistic, a considerable talent for painting, a delicate and highly trained ear for music, and a quick perception as to what is of value in literature, have led me to frequent at times the houses where one meets the best class of so-called Bohemians. They are interesting people whom one may cultivate or drop according to social convenience, and useful as living dictionaries of the intellectual fashions of the moment. Sometimes I have thought that their interest in my experiences (as related in conversation by myself) has been strangely apathetic, not to say inattentive, due perhaps (as indeed I have been told) to their admiration of my physical points. In explanation I may point out that I have been modelled in marble as Hercules. It was a birthday gift I devised for my second cousin (by marriage) the Duke of Haredale, and I gave the commission to that admirable French sculptor, Moreau.

My means, viewed in proportion to those of my friends, are at least sufficient. For, although my allowance is nominally but £2,000 a year, my father has such a morbid sense of the family honour that he is always ready to pay up the casual debts that spring from daily intercourse with the best of everything. And as he enjoys an income of quite £150,000 a year, mainly derived from coal mines in Wales, there really seems no reason why

I should not occasionally, indeed frequently, furnish him with an opportunity
for indulging in his harmless hobby of
keeping the family escutcheon clean.

I endeavour to keep in touch with
society journalism, and frequently entertain the editors of the more responsible
sporting and smart papers. The Press
being one of the glories of the age, I am
ever ready to foster it ; and though I care
not one straw for the personal puffs of
which I myself am so often the subject,
still I know that they give pleasure to my
friends, both at home and abroad.

As regards the literary style of these
pages, I desire to point out that its agree-
able flavour has been purveyed by a friend
of mine, an eminent critic who writes for
all the best daily and weekly papers both
in London and the provinces. I have
merely supplied the facts with such reflec-
tions and embroideries thereon as seemed
to me both necessary and graceful. He
has done the rest. Thus, if any adverse
criticisms of my book should appear—an

idea which I do not seriously entertain—the reader will understand that they are prompted either by professional jealousy or unfair rivalry, motives which, I am happy to think, have no place in the advanced and altruistic journalism of to-day.

And now, my reader, just before we plunge *in medias res*, I approach a subject which, if treated with candour, must also be handled with delicacy.

I desire to marry.

I desire to marry Katherine Clavering Gunter.

She is an American and a widow.

She is an enthusiastic golfer.

She is quite beautiful, especially in her photographs.

" SHE IS AN ENTHUSIASTIC GOLFER."

Since the day Carmody said, in the billiard-room at White's, that she reminded him of a blush rose whose outer petals were becoming touched with the tint of biscuits, I have cut him dead. Her beauty is to me full of freshness, especially at night.

She has a fortune of £2,000,000 sterling, and I love her with a very true and real love. That is to say, I love her with a perfectly balanced affection ; an affection based impartially on an estimate of her personal worth, an admiration for her physical charms, and an appreciation of her comfortable circumstances. I perceive that our union would further our respective interests in providing each of us with certain extensions of our present modes of living. I have long desired a place of my own in the country ; and Katherine, I know, wishes to move freely in smart circles without having to employ the services of impoverished dowagers. In many other ways I could be of assistance to Katherine. I could tell her how to wear her diamonds, for instance, a difficult art she has not yet acquired. She is inclined on the slightest provocation to decorate herself in exuberant imitation of a cut-crystal chandelier.

There are, however, difficulties.

Prominent among these is the fact, already mentioned, that she is an ardent golfer. Except during the season in town, she spends her year in golfing, either at St. Magnus or Pau, for, like all good Americans, she has long since abjured her native soil.

Now golf is a game that presents no attractions to me. I have never tried it,

MRS. GUNTER.

nor even held a golf-stick in my hand. A really good game, to my mind, must have an element, however slight, of physical danger to the player. This is the great whet to skilled performance. It is the condition that fosters pluck and self-reliance and develops our perception of the value of scientific play. It breeds a certain fearlessness that stimulates us not merely during the actual progress of the game, but unconsciously in the greater world where we play at Life with alert and daring opponents.

Now golf presents no such condition, and I despise it.

Once, by means of jocular query (a useful method of extracting such information as may not always be asked for bluntly), I gathered from Katherine that marriage with a keen golfer would probably be her future state ; and this admission, I confess, was extremely galling to me, the more so as I had just been entertaining her with a long summary of my own achievements in other games.

I little thought at the time that before many weeks had passed I should be playing golf as Heaven knows it was never played before.   And this is how it happened.

II

I DINE AT LOWCHESTER HOUSE

ONE warm, delicious evening late in July I was dining at Lowchester House. It was almost my last dinner engagement for the season, as all the world and his wife had suddenly got sick of the baking pavements and dusty trees of the great city, and were making in shoals for green fields or briny sea.

The ladies had just left us, and we men were preparing to enjoy the heavenly hour that brings cigarettes, coffee, and liqueurs in its wake. Through the wide-open French windows of the dining-room (which look out over St. James's Park) came softened sounds of busy traffic ; a ravishing odour of sweet peas stole in from the garden, and the moon gave to the trees and shrubs without those strange, grave tints that are her wonderful gifts to the night.

As a rule such an environment impresses and invigorates me pleasurably. I enjoy the journeys of the eye as it travels lightly over polished mahogany, glittering silver, and gleaming glass, noting here the deep red of the wine and roses, there the sunset-like effulgence of the hanging lamps, the vague outlines of the pictured oak walls, and the clearer groups of well-groomed men that sit in easy comfort under a blue canopy of lazily curling smoke. Or, as the glance passes to the scented garden without, noting the blue-green and silver wonderlands that the moon creates in the most commonplace and probably grimy of trees, and the quiver that the soft July wind gives to branch, leaf, and flower.

But to-night, somehow, such things had no charm for me.

And yet Lady Lowchester's dinner had been good. The cutlets, perhaps, a trifle uninteresting and the wine somewhat over-iced ; but, on the whole, distinctly good.

How, then, account for my mood ?

Katherine was of the party, but at the other end of the table from mine. A tall, well-built, massive man, good-looking, and possessed of an attractive smile, had taken her into dinner, and I have rarely seen two people so completely absorbed in each other.

Therein lay the sting of the evening.

I had eaten and drunk mechanically with eyes riveted, as far as good breeding would permit, on Katherine and her neighbour.

Who was he ?

I know everybody that one meets in London, either personally or by sight, yet I had never before come across this good-looking Hercules. I must find out.

He was talking to Lowchester as, leaving my chair, I carelessly joined the group at the other end of the table.

" Yes, I first held the open championship five years ago," I heard him say.

I pricked my ears. Of what championship was he speaking ?

" And again last year, I think ? " asked
Lowchester.

" Yes," replied Hercules.

I quickly inquired of my neighbour as
to what championship was under discussion.

" Why golf, of course," was the response. " That's Jim Lindsay, the finest
player living."

So that was it. No wonder Katherine
was so deeply absorbed during dinner.

I hated the man at once. I lost not a
moment. I darted my eyes across the
table, caught his, and stabbed him with
one of those withering knife-like glances
that only the descendants of the great
can inflict.

Then I discovered that he wasn't looking at me at all, but at one of my shirt
studs which had escaped from its button-
hole. He drew my attention to it. I
grunted out an ungrateful " Thanks ! "
and hated him the more.

Now, as a rule, after dinner—wherever I may be—I manage to hold the conversation. So much a habit has this become with me, that I can scarcely endure to hear another man similarly exploiting himself. Not, I am bound to say, that Lindsay was belauding his own prowess. But, what was worse, he appeared a centre of enormous interest to the men around him. They drew him out. They hung on his words. They gaped at him with reverential admiration. Truly golf must have made many converts during the last three years I had been in India. Bah! And I knew it to be such a childish game.

" I've taken a house close to the links at St. Magnus for the summer, Lindsay," Lowchester presently observed. " And as you tell me you're going there next month, you must let me put you up. There's lots of room, and Mrs. Gunter will be with us during August and September."

" I shall be delighted ; it will suit me exactly," replied Lindsay.

So Lowchester too had become a golfer! Lowchester—who used to live for hunting and cricket! Lowchester—the President of the Board of Education! Good heavens!

Presently we were all in the hideous gilded and damasked drawing-room; for Lowchester House is a sort of museum of the tawdry vulgarities of the early fifties.

The rooms were hot. That no doubt was the reason why presently Mrs. Gunter and the champion were to be seen hanging over the railing of a flower-laden balcony; but the heat could in no way account for their gazing into each other's eyes so frequently, or so raptly.

I seized on a slip of a girl in pink, led her close to the window, and in tones that I knew must be overheard by the occupants of the balcony, began to relate how I won the Lahore Polo Cup for my team in '92.

I was well under weigh and just reaching a stirring description of the magnificent goal I scored by taking the ball the

whole length of the ground, on a pony
that had suddenly gone lame, when
Katherine and the champion pointedly left
the window and proceeded to another and
more distant one.

So! My reminiscences bored them!
Polo was nothing if golf were in the air!

It was enough. I could stand no more.
I peevishly bade my hostess good night,
and passed through the rooms.

As I entered the great hall, which was
but dimly lit, my eyes encountered a
portrait of the famous (or infamous) Cardinal Smeaton, one of Lowchester's
proudest pictorial possessions. The great
Scotch prelate, I could have sworn, winked
at me.

I was moving on, when suddenly, close
to my shoulder, I heard the words, " I will
meet ye at St. Magnus! "

I started and turned. There was no
one near. I gazed fixedly at the portrait,
but never was marble more immovable. I
was about to investigate a recess and some
pillars, near me, when I observed a foot-

man at the hall door eyeing me with mild but interested scrutiny. He came forward with my coat and hat, and putting them on I passed listlessly into the courtyard and thence to St. James's Street, where I mechanically entered the doors of the Racing Club.

I rang the bell and ordered a brandy-and-soda.

III

THE CHALLENGE

THE Racing Club, as the reader
knows, is the smartest sporting club
in London, and the Inner Temple of the
popular game of " Bridge." But to-night
cards held no temptation for me ; and I
sat alone in the reading-room, chewing
the cud of a humiliation that was quite
novel to my experience.

The incident of the Cardinal's wink and
the unknown voice had already escaped
my memory, and I was rapt in rankling
memories of the unsatisfactory evening I
had spent.

To me, it was inconceivable that even
the finest exponent of a wretched game
like golf could oust an all-round sportsman
like myself from the circle of interest at a

dinner table. It was not so much that I had not been afforded an opportunity to talk, as that when I did I was listened to with a wandering and simulated attention, suggesting that the listeners were only waiting for me to stop. The moment I paused between two anecdotes, someone precipitately led the conversation away to a channel that had no possible interest for me.

Then Katherine had indubitably avoided and ignored me.

It has always been understood between us that if I am in a room with her, mine is the first claim on her attention. Yet, to-night, there was, if not an open rebellion, at least a new departure.

It was extremely galling, and I ordered a second brandy-and-soda.

Must I, then, take to golf in self-defence ?

Of course I could pick it up easily. There is no minor game that I have not mastered with ease, after about a week's hard application ; and to acquire the art of striking a ball from a certain distance into a hole presents no alarming difficulties to the adroit cricketer and practised polo player. Still, to go over, as it were, to the camp of the enemy, to apply myself to a game that I have openly and avowedly sneered at, was not altogether a pleasing prospect.

How it would tickle my pals at Hurlingham, Ranelagh, the Oval, and Lord's !

I took from the bookshelves the Badminton volume on Golf, and with a third brandy-and-soda applied myself to a rapid study of its contents. I admit that I was somewhat dismayed at the mass of printed matter and numerous diagrams that confronted me, but reflecting that I had often seen voluminous books on such trivial games as croquet or tennis, I concluded that the principle of sporting journalism is to make the maximum of bricks out of the minimum of straw.

I had not read more than three chapters when half a dozen men, including Lowchester and Lindsay, entered the room.

" My dear Jacky," said the former, " you left us very early to-night."

" Yes," I replied. " I found the atmosphere indoors a bit oppressive ; and I'm not as yet a convert to golf, your sole topic of discussion during the evening."

" You ought to try the game," said Lindsay. " There's more in it than outsiders imagine."

" ' Outsiders ' in what sense ? " I inquired, with an obvious courtship of a wordy wrangle.

" Oh ! only as regards golf, of course. For aught I know you may be a celebrity in many other branches of sport."

" I am," was on the tip of my tongue, but I repressed it.

I felt strangely antagonistic towards this man. A sort of magnetic antipathy (if I may be allowed such a seeming contradiction in terms) warned me that we should influence each other's lives in the future, and that to the detriment of one, if not both of us. In fact, I felt myself being drawn irresistibly towards the vulgar vortex of a " row " with him.

" Golf," I suddenly found myself asserting after one of those deadly pauses that give an altogether exaggerated significance to any casual remark that may break the silence, " Golf is a game for one's dotage."

" A period that sets in quite early in the lives of many of us," retorted Lindsay.

There was another pause. Lowchester was chuckling quietly. A club waiter with thin lips was grinning faintly.

" Which means ? " I asked, with an affectation of bored inattention.

" Well, it means," was the reply, " that to stigmatise as only suitable for one's dotage, a fine, healthy, outdoor sport, that employs skill and science, and exercises one's patience and temper as few other games do, suggests to my mind incipient dotage in common perception."

I did not understand this at first, so merely remarked, " Really," an ambiguous and useful word, which commits one to nothing.

But as I reflected on Lindsay's words, I perceived a deadly stab at my authority as a judge of sport. My blood tingled. I seized a fourth brandy-and-soda and drank it. It was Lowchester's, but I was only aware of this when the glass was empty. My lips compressed themselves. I recalled Katherine and the champion hanging over the balcony. The thin-lipped club waiter was loitering with an evident desire to overhear what else was to be said. Lowchester looked at me with gently humorous inquiry in his eyes. The others regarded me with the sphinx-like calm that is the ordinary expression of the average Englishman when he is thinking hard but not lucidly. I had, in fact, an audience, always to me an overpowering temptation.

" I'll tell you what I'll do," I said, in' the calm, deep tones born of a great determination. " After one week's practice on the St. Magnus links I'll play you a match on even terms, and I dare to hope lick your head off at your own game."

There was a pause of a moment. Then, as if to clear the oppressive air, a chorus of " Bravo, Old Jacky ! " broke out from the bystanders.

Only Lindsay was silent, barring, of course, the waiters.

" Well ? " I asked him.

" I accept, of course," said he ; " you leave me no alternative. But the whole scheme is absolutely childish, and, as I fear you will find, quite futile."

" I'll take my chance of that," I replied. " I can reach St. Magnus by August eighth, and on the fifteenth I'll play you."

" It's a match," cried Lowchester, and proceeded to enter it in a notebook. " Any stakes ? "

" I will privately suggest to Mr. Lindsay the stakes to be played for," I answered. " May I ask you to come with me for a moment ? "

Lindsay assented, and I led him to an adjoining room that was empty.

" The stake I suggest—and it must be

known to none but ourselves—is this. The winner of the match shall have the first right to propose matrimony to a certain lady. I mention no names. It is enough if we agree that neither of us shall propose to any lady whatsoever on or before August fifteenth, and that the loser shall further abstain from any such proposal till August twenty-second. This will give the winner a clear week's start, which really constitutes the stake. The subject is a delicate one," I hastily added, as I saw his surprise and evident desire to go further into the matter, " and I shall be obliged if you merely signify your assent or dissent, as the case may be."

With a certain bewildered yet half-amused air he replied, " I assent, of course, but—— "

" There is nothing more that need be said," I hurriedly interrupted, " except that I shall be glad if you will join me at supper."

For at one of my own clubs, when a stranger is introduced, even by another member, I trust I can ever play the host with tact and grace. I asked Lowchester and Grimsby to join us, and during supper I was able to recount the chief exploits of my life to the attentive audience that a host can always rely on.

IV

ST. MAGNUS

I LEFT London on August 6th, travelling by night to Edinburgh, and leaving the latter city at 9 a.m, on the 7th, reached St. Magnus a few minutes before noon. I had been recommended to try the Metropole Hotel, and accordingly took up my quarters there. It is quite near the St. Magnus Golf Club (for which I was put up at once as a temporary member), and is equally convenient to the links. Lord and Lady Lowchester were in their house, a stone's-throw from the hotel, and amongst their guests were Mr. Lindsay and Mrs. Gunter.

St. Magnus, as the golfing world knows, is situated on the east coast of Scotland, and is second only in importance as a golfing centre to St. Andrews, which, indeed, it closely resembles. It is a grim, grey old town, standing on bleak, precipitous cliffs that court every passing hurricane, and possessed in addition of a respectable perennial gale of its own. It is always blowing there. Indeed, I think a fair description of normal weather of St. Magnus would be " Wind with gales."

The ancient town boasts many ruins of once noble buildings. Cathedrals, castles, monasteries, colleges, and priories, that formed strongholds of Roman Catholicism before the Reformation, are now outlined only by picturesque and crumbling walls, held in a green embrace by the ever-sympathetic ivy, and preserved mainly to please the antiquarian or artistic eye.

And many the tales that are told of the ghostly occupants of these dead strongholds.

The hotel was tolerably comfortable, although under any conditions hotel life is, to me, a hateful business. The constant traversing of passages that lead

chiefly to other people's rooms ; the garrulous noisiness of the guests, the forced
yet *blasé* alacrity of the waiters, the com-
mercial suavity and professional geniality
of the proprietor, the absolute lack of
originality in the cook, the fact that one
becomes merely an easily forgotten number, these and a thousand other trivial
humiliations combine to render residence
in an hotel a source of irritation to the
nerves.

The club-house, however, was airy and
comfortably managed ; and the older
frequenters appeared to me to be good
types of Scotch county gentlemen, or
courteous members of the learned pro-
fessions. Some of the younger men I met
I did not quite understand. They had, to
begin with, quite extraordinary accents.
If you can imagine a native and strong
Scotch accent asserting itself in defiance
of a recently acquired cockney twang, you
have some idea of the strange sounds these
youths emitted. They were, however,
quite harmless ; and there really seemed

no reason why, if it pleased them, they should not garnish their Caledonian and somewhat bucolic dialogue with misplaced " Don't-you-knows," or denude it, in accordance with a long defunct phonetic fashion, of the letter " g." They were quite charmed with my prefix " Honourable," and duly acquainted me of such people of title as they had either seen at a distance or once spoken to at a railway station.

The general society of the place was considered " mixed " by the younger bloods of the town ; though, to my mind, these latter formed the most unpalatable part of the mixture. It numbered, to my surprise, half a dozen socially well-known people whom I frequently met in London. True, they kept pretty much to themselves and were not to be seen at the numerous tea-parties, female putting tournaments, badly cooked but pretentious dinners, and other social barbarities that were—Heaven help us !—considered *de rigueur* in this fresh seaside country town.

I, too, avoided all such festivities;
though from the moment I set foot in the
club, with name and condition advertised
on the notice board, I was inundated with
invitations; one of the many penalties, I
suppose, of being more or less of a sporting celebrity. I felt, indeed, much as a
great actor must when he goes " starring "
in the provinces.

There is, however, one charming section
of society in the grey old town, comprising
mainly those learned and cultured people
who own the city as their home. Mingl-
ing with these, some modern *littérateurs*
in search of bracing health give a vivacity
to the free exchange of ideas; whilst one
or two staid but intelligent clergymen
form a sort of moral anchor that holds
cultured thought to the needs of the world
rather than let it drift to the summer seas
of imagination. In such society I should
have been, of course, a welcome recruit;
but I was in St. Magnus for one purpose
only, and that was golf.

I have been writing calmly, but during

the days that followed my challenge to Lindsay, my brain was in a fever. I had stipulated for but one week's practice, and, consequently, though dying to handle the sticks (or " clubs " as I find I ought to call them), I had been debarred from more than a study of the game, as set forth in the various published works on the subject.

I had taken a suite of four rooms in the hotel. One was my sitting-room, another my bedroom, a third my servant's room, and the fourth I had fitted up as a golf studio. The latter is entirely my own invention, and I make no doubt that, after the publication of this volume, similar studios will become quite common institutions.

By arrangement with the proprietor, I had the room denuded of all furniture ; and it was understood between us that during my residence no one, not even a housemaid, should be permitted to enter the chamber, with, of course, the exception of myself and my servant. I had no desire that St. Magnus should know the extent to which I was laying myself out to defeat my opponent.

A strip of cocoa-nut matting, lightly strewn with sand, represented a teeing ground, whilst a number of padded targets, designed to receive the balls as I drove them, almost entirely covered the walls. A fourth of the floor was boarded in with sand, eighteen inches deep, to represent a bunker. The remainder I turfed to represent a putting green. I constructed a small movable grassy hillock which could be placed in the centre of the room for practice in " hanging " or " uphill " lies, and I imported whin-bushes, sods of long grass, etc., to represent the assorted difficulties that beset the golfer. By day, and until I was finished with the studio for the night, the windows were removed in case of accidents ; and altogether nothing was left undone that would conduce to complete and unobserved practice of the game.

In addition to this indoor preparation, I

decided to do at least two rounds daily, starting at daybreak. Allowing two hours for each round, this could easily be accomplished before 9 a.m., and St. Magnus would be little the wiser. Then, if my progress should prove unsatisfactory, starting out about 5 p.m., I could edge in a third almost unnoticed round.

I had six volumes by different writers on the game, and from these I gathered that instruction from a first-class professional was practically indispensable to the beginner. By dint of offering extremely liberal terms, I secured the services of the well-known professional Kirkintulloch, it being understood that he was to coach me more or less *sub rosâ*, and that in any case he was not to talk promiscuously of the extent to which I practised. I exhorted him to spare no expense—an arrangement he accepted with evident and spontaneous alacrity, selling me a number of his own unrivalled clubs at what I have since learnt were exorbitant prices. He also made a selection of other implements of the game from the best makers, that included fifteen beautifully balanced and polished clubs, four dozen balls, and several minor appliances, such as artificial tees, sponges, etc., to say nothing of a seven-and-sixpenny and pagoda-like umbrella. All these preparations were completed on the day of my arrival, and it was arranged that I should begin practice in deadly earnest at 4.30 on the following morning.

V

I BEGIN TO GOLF

THE morning of the 8th dawned with a warm flush of saffron, rose, and gold, behind which the faint purple of the night that was gone died into the mists of early morning. The pure, sweet air was delicious as the sparkling vapour that rises from a newly opened bottle of invigorating wine. The incoming tide plashed on the beach with lazy and musical kisses, and a soft, melodious wind was stirring the bending grasses that crowned the sand dunes on the outskirts of the links.

I inhaled the glorious air with the rapture of the warrior who sniffs the battle from afar.

[The literary grace of my esteemed journalistic colleague will be observed in the foregoing lines. "It was a ripping morning" was all I actually said to him. —J. W. W. G.]

Kirkintulloch was waiting for me at the first putting green.

I may say at once that during my entire stay in St. Magnus I never quite mastered this man's name. It became confused in my mind with other curious-sounding names of Scotch towns, and I addressed him promiscuously as Tullochgorum, Tillicoutry, Auchtermuchty, and the like. To his credit, be it said that after one or two attempts to put me right, he suppressed any claim to nominal individuality and adapted himself philosophically to my weakness; answering cheerfully to any name that greeted his surprised but resigned ears.

He was the brawny son of honest fisher folk. Of middle height, he was sturdily yet flexibly built. His hands were large and horny; his feet, I have no doubt, the same. At all events his boots were of ample proportions. He had blue eyes, with that alert, steady, and far-seeing gaze that is the birthright of folk born to look out over the sea ; sandy hair and moustache, and a ruddy colour that suggested equally sunshine, salt winds, and whisky. His natural expression was inclined to be sour, but on occasion this was dissipated by a quite genial smile. His manner and address had the odd deferential familiarity that belongs exclusively to the old-fashioned Scotch peasantry. His face I soon found to be a sort of barometer of my progress, for every time I struck a ball I could see exactly the value of the stroke recorded in the grim lines of his weather-beaten features. In movement he was clumsy, except, indeed, when golfing, for then his body and limbs became possessed of that faultless grace which only proficiency in a given line can impart.

" It's a fine moarn fur goalf," was his greeting.

" So I suppose," said I. " Where do we go ? "

" We'll gang ower here," he replied, as,

tucking my clubs under his arm, he led me in the direction of a comparatively remote part of the links.

As we went I thought it advisable to let him know that, although not yet a golfer, I could more than hold my own in far higher branches of sport. I told him that I was one of the best-known polo players of the day.

There was a considerable pause, but we tramped steadily on.

" Whaat's polo ? " said he, at length.

I gave him a brief description of the game.

" Aweel, ye'll no hae a hoarse to help ye at goalf."

" But, don't you see, Tullochgorum——"

" Kirkintulloch, sir."

" Kirkintulloch, that the fact of playing a game on ponies makes it much more difficult ? "

" Then whaat fur d'ye hae them ? "

" Well, it's the game, that's all."

" M'hm " was his sphinx-like response.

I felt that I had not convinced him.

I next hinted that I was a prominent cricketer, and, as a rule, went in first wicket down when playing for my regiment.

" Ay, it's a fine ploy fur laddies."

" It's a game that can only properly be played by men," I replied, with indignant warmth.

" Is't ? "

" Yes, is't—I mean it is." He had certain phrases that I often unconsciously and involuntarily repeated, generally with ludicrous effect.

The reader, of course, understands that I was not in any sense guilty of such gross taste as to imitate the man to his own ears. I simply could not help pronouncing certain words as he did.

" Aweel, in goalf ye'll no hae a man to birstle the ba' to yer bat ; ye'll just hae to play it as it lies."

" But, man alive," I cried, " don't you see that to hit a moving object must be infinitely more difficult than to strike a ball that is stationary ? "

" Ye've no bunkers at cricket," he replied, with irrelevant but disconcerting
conviction, adding, with an indescribable
and prophetic relish, " No, nor yet whins."

I could make no impression on this man,
and it worried me.

" I take it," I resumed presently, " that
what is mainly of importance at golf is a
good eye."

" That's ae thing."

" What's ae thing? "

" Yer e'e. The thing is, can ye keep it
on the ba' ? "

" Of course I can keep it on the ba'—
ball."

" We'll see in a meenit," he answered,
and stopped. We had reached a large
field enclosed by a wall, and here Kirkintulloch dropped the clubs and proceeded
to arrange a little heap of damp sand, on
which he eventually poised a golf ball.

" Noo, tak' yer driver. Here," and he
handed me a beautifully varnished implement decorated with sunk lead, inlaid
bone, and resined cord. " Try a swing "

—he said " swung "—like this," and, standing in position before the ball, he proceeded to wave a club of his own in semicircular sweeps as if defying the world in general and myself in particular, till suddenly and rapidly descending on the ball, he struck it with such force and accuracy that it shot out into the faint morning mist and disappeared. It was really a remarkably fine shot. I began to feel quite keen.

" Noo it's your turn," said he, as he teed a second ball, " but hae a wheen practice at the swung first."

So I began " addressing " an imaginary ball.

We wrestled with the peculiar flourishes that are technically known as " addressing the ball " for some minutes, at the end of which my movements resembled those of a man who, having been given a club, was undecided in his mind as to whether he should keep hold of it or throw it away. I wiggled first in one direction, then in another. I described eights and threes, double circles, triangles, and parallelograms in the air, only to be assailed with—

" Na, na ! " from Kirkintulloch.

" See here, dea it like this," he cried ; and again he flourished his driver with the easy grace of a lifetime's practice.

" I'll tell you what, Kirkcudbright——"

" Kirkintulloch, sir."

" Kirkintulloch, just you let me have a smack at the ball."

" Gang on then, sir. Hae a smack."

I took up position. I got my eye on the ball. I wiggled for all I was worth, I swung a mighty swing, I swooped with terrific force down on the ball, and behold, when all was over, there it was still poised on the tee, insolently unmoved, and Kirkintulloch sniffing in the direction of the sea.

" Ye've missed the globe," was his comment. " An' it's a black disgrace to a gowfer."

I settled to the ball again—and with a running accompaniment from Kirkintul-

"IT'S A BLACK DISGRACE TO A GOWFER"

loch of " Keep yer eye on the ba' ; up wi'
yer richt fut ; tak' plenty time ; dinna swee
ower fast "—I let drive a second time,
with the result that the ball took a series
of trifling hops and skips like a startled
hare, and deposited itself in rough ground
some thirty yards off, at an angle of forty-
five degrees from the line I had anxiously
hoped to take.

" Ye topped it, sir," was Kirkintulloch's
view of the performance.

" I moved it, anyhow," I muttered
moodily.

" Ay, ye did that," was the response ;
" and ye'll never move that ba' again, fur
it's doon a rabbit hole and oot o' sicht."

Nevertheless, I went steadily on, ball
after ball. They took many and devious
routes, and entirely different methods of
reaching their destinations. Some leapt
into the air with half-hearted and affrighted
purpose ; others shot along the ground
with strange irregularity of direction and
distance ; a number went off at right or
left angles with the pleasing uncertainty

that only a beginner can command ; whilst not a few merely trickled off the tee in sickly obedience to my misdirected energy. At length I struck one magnificent shot. The ball soared straight and sure from the club just as Kirkintulloch's had, and I felt for the first time the delicious thrill that tingles through the arms right to the very brain, as the clean-struck ball leaves the driver's head. I looked at Kirkintulloch with a proud and gleaming eye.

" No bad," said he, " but ye'll no do that again in a hurry. It was guy like an accident."

" Look here, Kirkincoutry," I said, nettled at last, " it's your business to encourage me, not to throw cold water ; and you ought to know it."

" Ma name's Kirkintulloch," he answered phlegmatically ; " but it doesna' maitter." (And this was the last time he corrected my errors as to his name.) " An' I can tell ye this, that cauld watter keeps the heed cool at goalf, and praise is a snare and a deloosion." Then with the ghost of a smile he added, " Gang on, ye're daein' fine."

The field was now dotted with some fifteen balls at such alarmingly varied distances and angles from the tee that they formed an irregular semicircle in front of us (one ball had even succeeded in travelling backwards); and as I reflected that my original and sustained purpose had been to strike them all in one particular line, I began to perceive undreamt-of difficulties in this royal and ancient game.

But I struggled on, and Kirkintulloch himself admitted that I showed signs of distinct, if spasmodic, improvement. At seven o'clock the driver was temporarily laid aside, and I was introduced in turn to the brassey, the iron, the cleek, the putter, and the niblick, the latter a curious implement not unlike a dentist's reflector of magnified proportions. The brassey much resembled the driver, but the iron opened out quite a new field of practice ; and my first attempts with it were rather in the nature of sod-cutting with a spade, varied at intervals by deadly strokes that left deep incisions on the ball.

As the clock of the parish church tolled the hour of 8.30, I returned to the hotel with an enormous appetite and a thought-ful mind.

VI

I CONTINUE PRACTICE

MY practice in the studio was not attended with that measure of success I had anticipated. The turf got dry and lumpy, and when, by my instructions, my servant watered it liberally, an old lady occupying the room immediately below intimated to the proprietor that her ceiling had unaccountably begun to drip, and that strange noises from the floor above deprived her of that tranquil rest for which she had sought the salubrious breezes of St. Magnus. A gouty dean, whose room adjoined the studio, also complained that sudden bangs and rattles on the walls, intermittent and varied but on the whole continuous, had so completely got on his nerves that residence in that quarter of the hotel had become an impossibility; whilst a number of other guests pointed out that to walk beneath my window was an extremely dangerous proceeding, as golf balls and even broken clubs flew out on them with alarming frequency and exciting results. I admit that I had a thoughtless habit of throwing offending clubs from the window in moments of extreme exasperation, but I exonerate myself of any intentional bombarding of my fellow-lodgers.

I myself suffered from this indoor zeal, for if a ball failed to strike one of the padded targets, and came in contact with the wall (as often happened), it would fly back boomerang-like to where I stood, not infrequently striking me so hard as to raise grisly lumps on various parts of my body. Once I invited Wetherby, my servant, to witness my progress, and during the few minutes of his incarceration with me he was driven to execute a series of leaps and springs to avoid the rapidly travelling and seemingly malignant ball. It struck him, I believe, three times, which some-

what militated against his evident desire
to pay me encouraging compliments, for
these latter he condensed into a meagre
and breathless " Wonderful, sir ! " as he
dashed from the studio with an alacrity
that was by no means constitutional with
him.

The miniature bunker also gave rise to
a certain amount of speculation on the
part of inmates of the hotel, for as I
generally practised on it facing the window,
casual loiterers below experienced brief but
disconcerting sandstorms, and the porters
and hall boys were kept busily occupied in
sweeping the unaccountably sanded pave-
ment.

I will not weary the reader with a description of my progress on the links from
day to day.   Suffice it to say that whilst I
really made wonderful strides, it became
borne in upon me, after five days' practice,
that under no possible conditions could I
hope to win the match I had set myself to
play.   For although I made many excellent, and even brilliant, strokes, I would

constantly " foozle " others, with the result
that I never got round the links under 100,
whereas Lindsay, I knew, seldom if ever
exceeded 90, and averaged, I suppose,
something like 86.

What, then, was I to do ? Give in ?
No.

I would play the match, and be beaten
like a man. There was a remote chance
that fortune might favour me. Lindsay
might be seedy—I knew he suffered at
times from the effects of malarial fever—
or I might by some unlooked-for provi-
dence suddenly develop a slashing game.

At all events I felt I must confide in
Kirkintulloch's ears the task I had set
myself.

Accordingly, on the morning of Satur-
day the 13th, I intimated to him, as we
started on our first round, that I had to
play my first match on the Monday.

" Ay," said he quite imperturbably.

" Yes," I resumed, " and rather an important one."

" Weel, I'll cairry for ye. Whaat time ? "

" Eleven o'clock," I replied ; and then, plunging *in medias res*, I added, " I'm playing a single against Mr. Lindsay, Mr. James Lindsay."

Kirkintulloch stopped dead, and gazed at me with blue-eyed and unceremonious incredulity.

" Jim Lindsay ! " he cried.

" Yes," I growled doggedly.

We proceeded to walk on, but, despite his impenetrable expression, I knew that Kirkintulloch was charged with violent emotion of some sort.

" What's he giein' ye? " he asked presently.

" What ? "

" What's yer hondicop ? "

" None. I'm playing him level."

" Weel, of a' the pairfect noansense——"

" Eh ? " I interrupted, with a certain dignity that was not lost on Kirkintulloch. But he again stopped dead, and for once in a way betrayed signs of some excitement.

" See here whaat I'm tellin' ye. He'll lay ye oot like a corp ! D'ye ken thaat ?

Forbye ye'll be the laughin'-stock o' the links. Ay, and *me* cairryin' for ye! I've pit up wi' a' the names ye've ca'd me—Tullochgorum, Tillicoutry, ay, and Auchtermuchty tae—but I'd hae ye mind I'm Wully Kirkintulloch, the professional. I've been in the mileeshy, an' I've done ma fowerteen days in the clink, but I'm no for ony black disgrace like cairryin' in a maatch the tail end o' which'll be Jim Lindsay scorin' nineteen up an' seventeen tae play."

I am not vain, but I confess that this speech, the longest oratorical effort that I remember Kirkintulloch to have indulged in, wounded my *amour propre*.

" If you don't wish to cairry—I mean carry—for me on Monday," I said, " there is no occasion for you to do so. I can easily get another caddie, and whoever does undertake the job will be paid one guinea."

I watched his features keenly as I said this, and though he in no wise betrayed himself by look or gesture, there was an

alteration in his tone when next he addressed me.

" It's like this, ye see," said he.   " I ken
ma business fine, and I ken a reel gentleman when I see yin, even when he's no
whaat ye might ca' profeecient as a goalfer,
an' I'm no sayin' I'll no cairry fur ye ; a' I
say is that ye're no tae blame me if Jim
Lindsay wuns by three or fower holes."

With this change of professional attitude
we proceeded on our way, and were soon
absorbed in the intricacies of the game.

That morning—how well I remember it !
—I was pounding away in one of the
deepest bunkers, filling my eyes, ears,
hair, and clothes with sand, exhausting
my vocabulary of language, and yet not
appreciably moving the ball.   I had played
seven strokes with ever-increasing frenzy.
With the eighth, to my momentary relief,
the ball soared from the sand to the grassy
slope above, only—oh, maddening game !
—to trickle slowly back and nest itself in
one of my deepest heel-marks.   Under
the impression that I was alone, I was

"I TURNED AND BEHELD MRS. GUNTER"

engaging in a one-sided, but ornate, conversation with the ball—for it is quite
extraordinary how illogically angry one
gets with inanimate objects—when, suddenly, from behind me came the clear
ring of a woman's laughter.

I turned and beheld Mrs. Gunter.

She was dressed in a tailor-made coat
and skirt of butcher blue, and wore a Tam
o' Shanter of the same colour. A white
collar and bright red sailor knot, adorable
white spats, and a white waistcoat completed the costume. Over her shoulder
she carried a cleek, and by her side was a
caddie bearing her other clubs. Her eyes
were sparkling with humour and enjoyment
of life, her cheeks glowed with the bright
fresh red that comes of sea air and healthy
exercise. Her enemies used to say she
was an adept at suitable complexions, but,
personally, I give the credit to the salubrious breezes of St. Magnus.

" Well ? " she cried, lustily (and she did
not pronounce it " wal.")   " How goes it ? "

" Tolerably," I replied, as I mopped

my perspiring brow. " You see me at present at my worst."

" Anna Lowchester is going to ask you to dinner on Monday to celebrate the great match. Mind you come. Say now, what are the stakes ? You know it's all over the town you're playing for something colossal. You'll have quite a crowd at your heels. And tell me why you avoid us all ? "

" I am here simply and solely to golf," I replied, with as much dignity as is possible to the occupant of a bunker that the merest novice could have avoided.

" Ye're keepin' the green waitin', sir," cried Kirkintulloch, as he appeared on the grassy slope in front of me.

" Then will you excuse me ? " I asked Mrs. Gunter, and settling down again I proceeded patiently to manœuvre under and round my ball. As I played the " eleven more," it rose in the air, and I left the bunker with a dignified bow to Katherine.

She passed on with a merry laugh and a wave of the hand, crying out as she watched the destination of my guttapercha, "You poor soul! You're bang into another."

And so I was. For a passing moment I almost hated Katherine.

It was quite true that I had avoided the Lowchesters. I was in no mood for society, still less did ·I care to meet Mr. Lindsay. True, I stumbled across him frequently in the club, but we instinctively limited our intercourse to a distant " Good morning," or a perfunctory " Good night."

Moreover, I was becoming extremely depressed.

Katherine's flippant and unsympathetic bearing during my vicissitudes in the bunker; the certainty that for the first time in my life I was about to be made a fool of ; the extraordinary difficulty I experienced in attaining to anything like an even sample of play ; and the half-pitiful, half-fearful regard in which I was held by the guests at the hotel, combined to rob life of the exhilaration that I had hitherto never failed to enjoy.

VII

I MEET THE CARDINAL

THE morning of Sunday the 14th broke with a dark and stormy scowl. The sea was lashed to a foaming lather by frantic gusts of easterly wind, and great black masses of clouds sped landward and piled themselves in ominous canopy over the grey and bleak-looking city. A seething and swirling mist all but enveloped the links, and the bending grasses of the dunes swayed and swished with every scourge of the salt-laden gale. Hard-driven and drenching rain swept in furious torrents across land and sea. The ground was as a swamp; the wet rocks, cold and streaming, stood as black targets for the fury of the mighty and resounding breakers that, spent in impotent attack, rose in vast clouds of spray.

Not a soul was to be seen out of doors.
The church bells, faintly and fitfully heard,
clanged their invitation to an irresponsive
town ; indoors, fires were already crack-
ling, pipes were lighted, magazines un-
earthed, and soon St. Magnus was court-
ing the drowsy comfort that snug shelter
from a raging storm ever induces.

I passed the time till luncheon in the
golf studio, but, out of consideration for
such Sabbatarian scruples as might possibly be entertained by the adjoining dean,
I merely trifled with a putter, and indeed
I had little heart even for that. The
clamour of the gong for the midday meal
was a welcome break to the black mono-
tony of the morning, and, descending to
the dining-room, I partook freely of such
northern delicacies as haggis (a really
excellent if stodgy dish), crab pies, and
oat cakes.

I then devoted a couple of hours to the
perusal of my books on golf, and copied
out, on a scale sufficiently small to be
easily carried in the pocket, a map of the

St. Magnus links for use on the morrow. A glance at this before each stroke would show me all the concealed hazards with which this admirably-laid-out course abounds. The idea is, I believe, a new one, and I present it gratuitously to all golfers who peruse this veracious history.

Dinner at the *Metropole* on Sundays is a more pretentious meal than on week-days. Game, cooked to a rag, figures on the menu, as also a profuse dessert of the cheaper and not quite ripe fruits of the season. Why this should be is not quite clear, as the golfer is robbed of his wonted exercise on a Sunday, and therefore should be lightly fed. It may be that in view of the spiritual rations dealt out to the im-mortal part of man that day, the hotel proprietor, in the spirit of competition which becomes his second nature, feels it incumbent on him to provide for the mortal interior with a prodigality that will bear comparison. Be that as it may, I did full justice to my host's catering, seeing it out to the bitter end, and banishing my depression with a bottle of the " Boy " and a few glasses of a port which was officially dated '64. It may have been that this wine had reached the sober age claimed for it, but to my palate, at least, it seemed to retain all the juvenile vigour and rough precocity of a wine still in its infancy.

About 10 p.m. I proceeded to the smoking-room and stretched myself luxuriously on a couch in front of a blazing fire, only to find that rest was not possible, and that I was the victim of what Scotch folk so aptly term the " fidgets." First, it appeared that I had been wrong to cross the right leg over the left, and I accordingly reversed the position. The momentary ease secured by this change was succeeded by a numbness in the right elbow which demanded that I should turn over on my left side. But this movement led to a stiffening of the neck, unaccountable yet unmistakable, and I turned for relief to the broad of my back, only to start a sudden and most irritating tickling in the sole of my right foot. I endured these tortures in silence for a time, attributing them, rightly, I imagine, to the fact that I had had no exercise during the day. The culminating point, however, was reached when the tickling sensation incontinently transferred itself to the back, suggesting to my now maddened imagination two prickly-footed scorpions golfing between my shoulder blades. I scraped myself, after the manner of cattle, against the wooden arms of the couch without obtaining appreciable relief, and finally sprang to my feet with a bound that startled a number of somnolent old gentlemen into wide-awake and indignant observation.

I must have exercise.

I drew aside one of the curtains and looked out on the night. The storm had somewhat abated, and the moon sailed brilliantly at intervals through the black and scudding clouds.

I decided on a walk, despite the weather and the lateness of the hour. I made for my room, arrayed myself, with Wetherby's assistance, in top-boots, mackintosh, and sou'-wester, and thus armoured against the elements I sallied forth into the wild and eerie night.

As I left the doors of the hotel eleven solemn clangs from the parish church warned me of the approaching " witching hour of night."

The town, despite the fact that most of the town councillors are interested in the local gas company, is extremely badly lighted ; and by the time I had passed the hospitable and inviting rays that streamed from the doors and lamps of the club-house, I was practically in the dark.

I took the road that extends along the cliffs to the harbour, at times compelled to probe for and feel my way, at times guided by fitful splashes of moonlight. And the scene when the moon chose to break through her pall-like veil was superb. Before me, in cold and inky outline, stood the ruined towers and windows of cathedral and castle ; to the left the sea, in a riot of black and white, still hurled itself with un-abated fury against the adamant rocks and along the unresisting beach. The sky was an ever-changing canopy of black and sullen grey, sparsely streaked with rifts of gleaming silver. Great trees bent and creaked on my right, flinging, as in a perspiration of midnight fear, great drops on the roadway below, sighing and screaming as if the horrid winds were whispering ghastly tales to their sobbing and tear-stained leaves, tales not to be breathed in the light of day.

A profound sense of awe stole over me as, riveted by the scene each passing glimpse of the moon revealed, I stood my ground from time to time, and held my breath in a frame of mind quite foreign to my experience.

[Here again will be observed the literary elegance of my gifted colleague. The preceding paragraphs have been evolved from my simple statement, " It was a beastly wet night."—J. W. W. G.]

So slow had been my progress that almost an hour must have passed before I reached the gates of the ruined castle. As

I stood gazing up at the weather-beaten heights, faintly limned against the flying clouds, I became conscious of a sudden and strange atmospheric change. The gale inexplicably died ; the trees hushed themselves into a startling silence ; the moon crept behind an enormous over-hanging mountain of clouds ; and warm, humid, and oppressive air replaced the sea-blown easterly winds. A great and portentous stillness prevailed around me, broken only by a dull moaning—as of a soul in agony—from the sea.

The effect was awful.

I strained eyes and ears in an ecstasy of anxiety. I knew not what was awaiting me, and yet knew of a certainty that I was about to face some strange revelation of the night.

Above all a great and overpowering horror of the dead was in me.

I tried to retrace my steps and found myself immovable, a living and breathing statue clutching the iron bars of the castle gate, waiting—waiting for what ?

Could it be that I, this quivering, power-less, quaking creature, was indeed John William Wentworth G——

Crash!—Crash!!

Within, as it seemed to me, a few feet of where I stood, a mighty blue and blinding flame shot out from the massive pile of clouds, firing sea and land with livid and fearsome light. Crash upon crash, roar upon roar of such thunder as I pray I may never hear again, struck up into the heights of the heavens and down again to the resounding rocks and ruins that fronted me. They broke in deafening awful blows upon my ear and stunned me. In a moment of utter collapse I fell through the gate, and lay with closed eyes on the soaking turf within. But closed eyes had no power to keep out such burning fire, and each blue flash came piercing through the eyelids.

Gasping, and with a supreme and almost superhuman effort, I staggered to my feet and opened my eyes in bewildered and fearful expectation.

And what was the wild, weird thing I saw?

At the entrance to the castle, just beyond the draw-bridge, holding aloft a wrought-iron lamp of ecclesiastical design that burnt with a sputtering and spectral flame, stood the red-robed figure of a ghostly cardinal!

With a wildly beating heart I recognized at a glance the face of the long dead Cardinal Smeaton, the Cardinal whose portrait had arrested my eyes at Lowchester House!

VIII

THE CARDINAL'S CHAMBER

"I SHIVERED IN EVERY LIMB"

I SHIVERED in every limb, and a cold beady dew sprang out on my temples as I stood with eyes riveted on the spectral figure before me. The light from the lamp fell on the left side of the Cardinal's head with a weird and Rembrandt-like effect, revealing a face with the tightly stretched grey-blue skin of the dead, and a fiercely flashing eye that seemed to divine the fear and horror that possessed me. Never to my dying day shall I forget that awful burning eye, glowing in what seemed to be the face of a corpse. I saw in its depths a grim triumph, a sardonic rapture, and a hideous relish of the blind horror betrayed in my blanched and streaming face.

The faded *vieux-rose* robes of the Cardinal (through which, as it seemed to me, I could faintly see the grey walls of the castle) only served to heighten the unearthly pallor of the face.

I swayed to and fro in the weakness of a sudden fever. My dry lips bit the air. I raised a hand to my eyes to shut out the appalling sight; but of strength I had none, and my arm dropped nervelessly to my side. Presently—and I almost shrieked aloud as I saw it—his thin but redly gleaming lips moved, displaying a set of yellow and wolfish teeth.

"Come," he said, in hollow yet imperious tones; "it's a sair nicht, and there is shelter within."

"No! no!" I cried, in an agony of fearful apprehension. But even as I spoke I moved mechanically towards him, and no words can convey the horror with which I realized my unconscious advance.

The wind shrieked out anew, and a deluge of sudden rain beat down from the clouds above.

Nearer and nearer I drew, with staring eyes and parted lips, until, as I found myself within a few feet of the ghastly thing, I stretched out my hands towards it in mute and awe-stricken appeal.

In a moment the Cardinal's right hand shot out, and fixed an icy grasp on my left wrist. I shivered violently to the very marrow, stricken powerless as a little child. The calm of despair came to me. I moved as in a dream. I was conscious that I was absolutely in the power of a spirit of the dead.

A flash of lightning and a crash of thunder heralded our entrance beneath the portcullis gate of the ruins.

I dared not look at the Cardinal's face. My eyes I kept on the ground, and I noted in a dreamily unconscious way the yellow pointed shoes of my ghostly guide

as they slipped noiselessly from beneath
the flowing draperies. At times, through
his robes, I seemed to see glimpses of a
white skeleton, and my teeth chattered
loudly at the fearsome sight.

We had passed into the shelter of the
archway that leads to the open courtyard
of the castle, and on our right was a door-
way that opened into a dark and damp
recess.

Into this I was dragged, the bony
fingers of His Eminence still eating into
my throbbing wrist. At the distant end
of the recess the Cardinal pressed with the
open palm of his disengaged hand (for he
had set down the lamp) a keystone that
stood out an inch or so from the dripping
and moss-grown wall. In immediate answer to the pressure a great block in the
wall moved slowly inwards, revealing a
faintly lit staircase with a spiral descent,
evidently cut through solid rock. This
we descended, I half slipping, half dragged,
until at length we reached a chamber
lighted almost brilliantly with flickering

tapers, and furnished in what had once no doubt been sumptuous fashion.

Here the Cardinal closed the old oak and iron-studded door with a clang that resounded eerily behind me, and releasing my almost frozen wrist, seated himself with grave dignity in a carved chair of ancient and pontifical design.

I looked around me.

The chamber, some sixteen feet square, was vaulted in the manner of a crypt, and the roofing stones were painted in frescoes, each panel representing the coat-of-arms of some old Catholic family. The walls were hung with faded and moth-eaten tapestry, depicting scenes of wild carousal, wherein nymphs, satyrs, and bacchantes disported themselves with cup and vine-leaf to the piping of a figure that closely resembled his satanic majesty. In one corner of the room stood a *prie-dieu*, and above it a broken and almost shapeless crucifix, overgrown with a dry, lichen-like moss, and shrouded in cobwebs. In front of this, depending from the roof, swung an incense burner that emitted a faint green light and an overpowering and sickly aromatic vapour.

The floor was of plain, dull granite in smooth slabs, from which a cold sweat seemed to exude. The four chairs were of carved oak, with the high pointed backs of the cathedral stall, and on either side of each tall candles burned with sepulchral flames of yellow and purple.

In the centre was a small square table of oak, the legs of which were carved to represent hideous and snake-like monsters, and on it stood a skull, a book, and an hour-glass.

A sense of disconcerting creepiness was diffused throughout the chamber by the fact that it was overrun by numerous immense spiders, some red, some yellow, and others black. Indeed, so ubiquitous were these horrid creatures that once or twice I fancied I saw them running up and down the faint white lines of His Eminence's skeleton. But as the Cardinal himself evinced no signs of inconvenience

from these intimate and presumably tickling recreations, I concluded that they were
the fevered creations of my own heated
imagination.

Another strange thing was that through
the apparently material appointments of
the chamber, I could dimly, yet undoubtedly,
see the rough, dripping walls of the solid
rock ; and when, by the Cardinal's invitation, I seated myself on one of the chairs
facing him, I was conscious that I passed,
as it were, through it, and actually sat
on a wet stone, to which the chair was
seemingly but a ghostly and ineffective
covering.

There was a certain sense of relief in
this, for I argued that if my surroundings
had no substance, no more probably had
the Cardinal or the spiders. And yet a
glance at my wrist showed me the livid
imprints of His Eminence's bony fingers.

Presently I ventured to let my gaze fall
on the Cardinal, and was somewhat re-
lieved to note in his otherwise inscrutable face a distinct twinkle of amusement.

The corners of his lips suggested an appreciation of humour; and his eyes betrayed an ill-concealed merriment as, from time to time, I shifted uneasily on my seat in an endeavour to find the driest part of it.

I was reflecting on the strange calm that was gradually coming to me—for, oddly enough, I began to lose the overwhelming sense of terror that a few minutes before had possessed me—when my ghostly companion broke the silence, speaking in profound and dignified tones.

" When the moon is at the full, gude sir, and eke the tide is low, a body that spiers within the castle gates maun e'en be guest o' mine."

I did not quite understand this, but feeling it to be an announcement that demanded a response of some sort, I replied respectfully, if somewhat feebly, " Quite so."

That my answer did not altogether satisfy His Eminence seemed apparent, for after regarding me in contemplative silence for a moment he uttered the portentous words, " I'm tellin' ye ! "

I quite felt that it was my turn to say something, but for the life of me I could not focus my ideas. At length, with much diffidence, and with a distinct tremor in my voice, I murmured, " I fear I'm inconveniencing Your Eminence by calling at so late an hour."

At this the Cardinal lay back in his chair and laughed consumedly for the space of at least a minute.

" Gude sake ! " cried he at last. " The Sassenach is glib eneuch tae jest ; wi' deeficulty nae doot, as indeed befits the occasion ! "

It will be observed that my ghostly prelate spoke in broad Scotch, much as Kirkintulloch did, with, however, the difference that is lent to speech by cultured cadences and a comparatively exhaustive vocabulary. From the unexpected laughter with which my diffident remark had been received, I instinctively derived a cue. It seemed to me that the Cardinal appreciated the subdued effrontery that I now perceived in my words, though at the moment of their utterance, Heaven knows, I only intended to convey extreme humility and deference. So I hazarded a question.

" May I ask," I ventured, with deferential gravity, " what keeps Your Eminence up so late ? "

" Hech ! sir," was the reply. " That's what liteegious folk would ca' a leadin' question. Forbye, I'm no just at leeberty tae tell ye. Ye see, folk maun work oot their ain salvation, and it's no permitted to the likes o' me, a wanderer in the speerit, to acquaint mortal man wi' information as to the existence of heaven, hell, purgatory, or—or otherwise."

" Then," I timidly pursued, with a good deal of hesitation, and beating about the bush to find appropriate terms, " I presume I have the—the—honour of addressing a—a spirit ? "

" Jist that," responded the Cardinal, with a sort of jocose cordiality that was very reassuring and comforting.

His whole manner had incredibly changed, and was now calculated to set one at ease, at least as far as might be between one representative of the quick and another of the dead. So conspicuously was this the case that I soon found the fear and horror that at first had so completely overwhelmed me replaced by an absorbing and inquisitive interest.

IX

HIS EMINENCE AND I

" FROM the exalted ecclesiastical position held in life by Your Eminence," I presently found myself saying, " I feel justified in assuming that you are now enjoying the well-merited reward of residence in heaven."

The Cardinal eyed me shrewdly for a moment, and eventually replied in diplomatic but evasive terms—

" I'm obleeged for the coampliment, be it merited or otherwise ; but I'm na' disposed tae enter into ony personal exposeetion of my speeritual career. This, however, I'm constrained to tell ye, that ninetenths o' the clergy and pious laity of a' creeds, at present in the enjoyment o' life, will be fair dumbfounded when they shuffle

off this moartal coil, and tak' possession
of the immortal lodgin' provided for them
—lodgin's that hae scant resemblance to
the tangible Canaans of their quasi-re-
leegious but business-like imaginations.
Catholic and Protestant alike, they're a'
under the impression that releegion is a
profession for the lips and no' for the lives.
As for Presbyterians, aweel! they'll find
oot in guid time the value o' their dour
pride in hard and heartless piety. They
ken fine hoo tae mak' a bargain in siller
wi' their neebors, but the same perspicacity
'll no' avail them when it comes tae——
but Hoots! It's nae business o' mine."
Then, as if to change the subject, he added,
" I suppose ye've read a' aboot me in the
Histories of Scotland ? "

" Well," I replied, " I've read a good
deal about Your Eminence. I've often
pictured you sitting at a window of the
castle, watching with grim enjoyment
young Dishart burning at the stake."

It was an unwise remark to make, and I
saw the Cardinal's eye flash balefully.

" Yer speech," he answered slowly and with dignity, " is no' in the best of taste, but it affords me an opportunity of explaining that misrepresented circumstance. Ye see, from a lad upwards, I was aye fond of a bonfire, and what for was I no' to watch the bonny red flames loupin' up forenenst the curlin' smoke ?   Was that pleasure tae be denied me, a' because a dwaibly manbody ca'd Dishart was frizzlin' on the toap ?   Na, na, guid sir, I was glowering at the bonny flames, no' at Dishart.   I saw Dishart, nae doot ; still, and there had no' been a fire, I wouldna hae lookit."

During this speech my attention had been somewhat distracted by the creepy spectacle of two spiders, one red, one black, fighting viciously on one of His Eminence's white ribs.   The sight affected me so disagreeably that I felt constrained to inform the Cardinal of the unpleasant incident.

" Your Eminence will excuse me," I said respectfully, " but I see two poisonous-looking spiders diverting themselves on one of your ribs, the lowest but one on the left side."

The Cardinal smiled, but made no movement. " I'm much obleeged," he responded, with grave amusement. " Nae doot ye're ruminatin' that sich internal gambols are no' compatible wi' the residence in heaven ye were guid eneuch to credit me wi'." Then, with a certain air of resigned weariness, he added, " Dinna mind them, they're daein' nae herm ; ye canna kittle a speerit, ye ken."

My seat was so extremely wet, and the damp was now penetrating my clothes in such an uncomfortable manner, that I resolved to assume an erect position at any cost. I may mention that we have rheumatism in our family. I cast about in my mind for a suitable reason for rising, and after some hesitation rose, remarking—

" Your Eminence will excuse me, but I feel it fitting that I should stand whilst a prelate of your exalted rank and undying

"AY! YE'RE GUY WET"

x

94

celebrity " (this last, I thought, under the circumstances, a particularly happy inspiration) " is good enough to condescend to hold intercourse with me."

" Ay ! Ye're guy wet," replied the undying celebrity, with a grasp of the situation that I had not looked for.

I stood shifting about on my feet, conscious of a rather painful stiffness in my joints, and wondering when and how this extraordinary séance would draw to a close, when the Cardinal, who had been lost for a time in the silence of a brown study, suddenly leaned forward in his chair and addressed me with an eager intensity that he had not displayed before.

" I'm gaun tae tell 'ee," said he, " what for I summoned ye here this nicht.   Here ! " he exclaimed, and rising he indicated the vaulted chamber with an imposing sweep of his gaunt arms and bony fingers, " Here ! In this ma *sanctum sanctorum.*"

He paused and eyed me steadily.

" I'm delighted, Your Eminence," I murmured feebly.

" Ye'll be mair than delighted, I'm thinkin'," he continued, " when ye ken ma purpose ; the whilk is this. The moarn's moarn ye're playin', an I'm no mistaken, a match at goalf agin a callant ca'd Jim Lindsay ? "

" That is so," I answered, in vague bewilderment at this sudden reference to a standing engagement in real life. For a moment a wild doubt swept over me. Was I living or dead ? The dampness of my trousers gave a silent answer in favour of the former condition.

" Aweel ! " resumed the Cardinal, " I'd have 'ee ken that he's a descendant in the straight line o' ane o' my maist determined foes—ye'll understand I'm referrin' tae sich time as I was Cardinal Airchbishop o' St. Magnus in the flesh—and ony blow that I can deal tae ane o' his kith is a solace to ma hameless and disjasket speerit. Noo, in ma day, I was unrivalled as a gowfer ; there wasna ma equal in the land. Nane o' the coortiers frae Holyrood were fit tae tee a ba' tae me. It's a fac'. And here—here ma gentleman!" (and the Cardinal sank his voice to the low tremulous wail of a sepulchral but operatic spectre, and his eyes gleamed with the sudden and baleful light that had first so riveted my gaze), " ahint the arras in this verra chamber is concealed ma ain bonny set of clubs!"

He paused and scrutinised my face to observe the effect of this announcement. I accordingly assumed an expression of intense interest.

" Noo," he continued, his eyes blazing with vindictive triumph, " I'm gaun tae lend ye this verra set o' clubs, an' I guarantee that an ye play wi' them ye'll win the day. D'ye hear that ?"

" It is extremely good of you," I murmured hurriedly.

" Hoots! It's mair for ma ain gratification than for yours. In addeetion I'll be wi' ye on the links, but veesible to nane but yersel. Ye'll wun the day, and fair humeeliate the varmint spawn o' my ancient foe ; and, eh! guid sir, but these auld bones will fair rattle wi' the pleesure o't! Will 'ee dae't?"

"I will," I solemnly replied. What else could I have said?

"Then hud yer wheest whiles I fetch the clubs."

With this His Eminence turned to the tapestry behind him, and, drawing it aside, disclosed a deep and narrow cavity in the rock. From this he extracted, one by one, a set of seven such extraordinarily un-wieldy-looking golf clubs that I felt it in me to laugh aloud. Needless to say I indulged in no such folly. I examined them one by one with apparent interest and simulated appreciation, as, fondling them lovingly, my companion expatiated on their obviously obsolete beauties. A strange and almost pathetic enthusiasm shone in his eyes.

"Nane o' yer new-fangled clubs for me," cried the Cardinal; "they auld things canna be bate. Tak' them wi' ye back tae whaur ye bide; bring them to the links the moarn's moarn, and as sure as we

stand here this nicht—or moarn, fur the
brak o' day is close at haun'—I'll be wi'
ye at the first tee, tae witness sic a game o'
gowf as never mortal played before. But
eh! guid sir, as ye'd conserve yer body
and soul frae destruction and damnation,
breathe nae word o' this queer compact
tae man, wumman, or bairn. Sweer it,
man, sweer it on this skull!"

His bloodless hands extended the grinning skull towards me, and I, repressing an
involuntary shudder, stooped and kissed it.

A gleam of malignant triumph again lit
up his face as I took the oath. Then he
seized the weird-looking clubs, and, caress-
ing them with loving care, muttered to
himself reminiscences of bygone years.

"Ay, fine I mind it," he cried, " when
young Ruthven came gallivantin' tae
St. Magnus, and thocht his match was
naewhere tae be foond. We had but five
holes in thae days, ye ken, and ilka yin a
mile in length. Hech, sir! what a match
was that! I dinged him doon wi' three up
and twa tae play. Ye'll no be disposed to

gie me credence, but it's a fact that I did yin hole in seventeen!"

"That was unfortunate," I replied, mistaking his meaning.

"Ay, for Ruthven," was his quick and peevish rejoinder. "For he took thirty-seven and lost the hole."

I had not grasped that he considered his own score extremely good.

"Of course I meant for Ruthven," I stammered, with the vague and silly smile of clumsy apology.

"Ye didna," replied His Eminence; "but I'm no mindin'. Ruthven, wi' a' his roughness, was an affectit callant in thae days, and rode his horse atween ilka shot. He moonted and dismoonted seeventy-fower times in three holes that day." And the Cardinal chuckled loud and long.

He related many other tales of his prowess with great gusto and enjoyment. We were now on such unaccountably familiar terms that I ventured to tell him of the marvellous goal I had won, playing for the Lahore Polo Cup in '62, when, of a sudden, he interrupted me, crying out—

" The oor is late ! Ye maun hae a sleep. Awa ! man, awa ! For ony sake, tak' the set and awa ! "

And indeed I needed no second invitation ; so, seizing the seven weird clubs, I made a low obeisance to His Eminence, and turning, found the door behind me open. I fled up the stone-cut staircase, passed like a flash through the recess to the archway, and, with a cry of such delight as surely never greeted mortal ears, I hailed the faintly dawning day. With the joy of a captive set free, or the rapture of one who has returned from a living tomb to bustling life, I inhaled the precious air in deep lung-filling draughts.

The storm had passed, the sea was calm, birds twittered in the gently whispering trees, the world was waking, and I was on its broad earth again.

But my thoughts were chaos. My brain refused to work. I had but one desire, and that was to sleep. In wretched plight

I reached the doors of the hotel, where the astounded night porter eyed me, and more particularly the hockey-stick-like clubs, with a questioning surprise and bated breath.

I made him bring me a stiff glass of hot whisky and water. This revived me somewhat, and telling him to warn my servant not to call me before 10 a.m., I staggered to my room, flung the clubs with a sudden, if scarcely surprising, abhorrence into a wardrobe, got out of my dripping clothes into welcome pyjamas, and, pulling the bedclothes up to my chin, was soon at rest in a dreamless sleep.

X

THE FATEFUL MORNING

I WOKE to find sunshine streaming in at the windows, a cloudless sky without, and my servant Wetherby busily occupied over his customary matutinal duties.

With a sudden flash of memory I recalled the weird scene of the night that was gone, only, however, to dismiss it as an unusually vivid dream. For a time I felt quite sure it was nothing more. But presently, as my eye fell on the empty glass that had held the hot whisky and water, I began to experience an uneasy doubt.

Ah! Now I remembered!

If it were a dream, there would be no clubs in the wardrobe.

I lit a cigarette, and asked Wetherby the time.

"Ten o'clock, sir," was the reply; "and you've no time to lose, sir. The match is at eleven."

I sprang from bed, and casually opened the wardrobe.

Good heavens! It was no dream! There they were! Seven of the queerest clubs that antiquarian imagination could conceive.

So it had actually happened! I had been the guest of Cardinal Smeaton's ghost, and had entered into a compact with him to use his ridiculous clubs in order that he might revel in a trumpery revenge on the house of Lindsay.

Be hanged if I would! I remembered vaguely that in law an oath exacted from a party by threat or terror was not held to be binding, and I determined to ignore my unholy bond with the shadowy prelate. I would play with my own clubs and be defeated like a man.

I jumped into my bath. The pure

morning air swept through the open window, the sunlight streamed in on the carpet and danced in circles of glancing gold in the clear cold water of the bath, and a glow of health and vigour (despite the late hours I had kept) sent the blood tingling through my veins. Indeed, what with the ordinary routine of dressing, my servant's presence, the hum of life that came from the links, the footsteps of housemaid and boots hurrying past my door, and generally my accustomed surroundings, I found it all but impossible to believe that I had really gone through the strange experiences of a few hours ago.

Yet, undoubtedly, there stood the clubs. Curious and perplexing ideas flashed through my mind as I dressed, ideas that clashed against or displaced each other with kaleidoscopic rapidity.

Was such an oath binding ? Was the whole incident a dream, and the presence of the clubs an unexplainable mystery ? Was there mental eccentricity on either side of my family ? Had my father, the son of a hundred earls (or, more correctly, of as many as can be conveniently crowded into a period of a hundred years), transmitted to me some disconcerting strain in the blue blood that filled my veins ; or, had my mother, with her less important but more richly gilt lineage, dowered me with a plebeian taint of which absurd superstition was the outcome ?   Or had the combination of both produced in myself a decadent creature abashed at his first introduction to the supernatural ? How could I tell ?   Was there really a spectral world, and I its victim ?   Was I reaping the harvest of years of cynical unbelief ?   Was I myself ?   And, if not, who was I ?

I gave it up.

I determined to ignore and if possible to forget entirely my creepy adventure in the vaults of the ruined castle.   In this endeavour I was assisted by the pangs of healthy hunger.   There is something so homely, so accustomed, so matter-of-fact in a good appetite, that I felt less awed

by the unwilling oath I had taken, when
Wetherby announced that an omelette and
a broiled sole were awaiting me in the
next room.

I was endeavouring to force into my tie
and collar one of those aggravating pins
that bend but never break, and alternately
wounding my neck and forefinger in the
process, when, through the open window,
my eye fell on a dense and apparently
increasing crowd that surged on the links
behind the first teeing ground. A dozen
men held a rope that must have measured
close on a hundred yards, and behind it
the entire population of the town seemed
to be gathering.

What could it be? Possibly a popular
excursion, a public holiday, or a big professional match.

I asked Wetherby.

" I understand, sir," replied that phleg-
matic youth, " the crowd is gatherin' in
anticipation of your match with Mr.
Lindsay, sir."

" Oh! Is it?" I murmured vaguely.

" It's been talked about considerable, sir."

" Has it ? " was all the comment I could muster.

I was appalled at the sight. There was a horribly expectant air in the crowd. Their faces had that deadly going-to-be-amused expression that I have seen in the spectators at a bull fight in Spain. Many eager faces were turned in the direction of my windows, and I shrank instinctively into the seclusion that a muslin curtain affords.

That dim recollection of the bull fight I had seen in Cadiz haunted me.

Was I to be a golfing bull ?

Or was Lindsay ?

Was I to be the golfing equivalent of the wretched horse that eventually is gored to death, to the huge delight of thousands of butcher-souled brutes ?

Well, if so, they would see a bold front. I'd show no craven spirit.

I began to wonder if the seven queer clubs had the properties that the Cardinal claimed for them. And then an idea seized me. I would have them near me on the links, and if the game went desperately against me I'd put them to the test.

" Wetherby," I said, as I put the finishing twist to my moustache, " I should like you to carry these odd-looking clubs round the links in case I want them. I don't propose to use them, but it is just possible that I might."

" Yes, sir."

I handed him a capacious canvas bag. I had purchased three similar bags from Kirkintulloch by his advice, one for fine weather, a second for wet, and the third (which I now gave Wetherby) an immense one for travelling. Kirkintulloch had informed me that without these my equipment as a golfer was incomplete.

" I don't wish them to be seen, unless it happens that I decide to use them, so you needn't follow me too closely," I added.

" I understand, sir."

" But you'll be at hand should occasion arise."

" Certainly, sir."

And shouldering the seven unwieldy weapons, Wetherby left the room with a twinkle in his eye that I had never remarked before.

I took another furtive glance at the crowd, and my heart gave a leap as I saw way being made for a party that included Mrs. Gunter and Lord and Lady Lowchester.

I passed mechanically to my sitting-room and sat down to breakfast.

I began to eat.

Thanks to the discipline of daily habit, my hands and jaws performed their accustomed tasks, but my mind was in a condition alternately comatose and chaotic, so much so that it was a matter of surprise to me when I found my eyes resting on the bones of my sole and the sloppery trail of a departed omelette.

I drained my coffee to the dregs and lit a cigarette.

I began to feel a sense of importance. The knowledge that one's personality is of interest to a crowd is always stimulating, but I was haunted with the uncomfortable reflection that sometimes a crowd is bent on jeering, not to say jostling. Ah! if only I could manage that those who came to laugh remained to—well to laugh at the other man.

Presently the door opened and Wetherby presented himself, with the smug deference for which I paid wages at the rate of sixty pounds a year.

" Mr. Lindsay's compliments, sir, and if you are ready, sir, he is."

" I am coming," I replied, as, passing a napkin across my lips, I pulled myself together for the impending ordeal.

As I walked through the hall of the hotel I saw that the entire domestic staff had gathered together to witness my exit. There was an uncomfortable sort of suppressed merriment in their faces that was not encouraging. The waiter who attended me at meals had the refined impertinence to blush as I passed. The boots seized his lips with two blacking-black hands, as if to deny his face the satisfaction of an insubordinate smile. A beast of a boy in buttons winked, and the general manager bowed to me with a deference so absurdly overdone as to be extremely unconvincing.

I passed through the folding doors, and stood on the steps of the hotel facing the crowd.

A tremendous cheer greeted me. When I say "cheer," possibly I don't quite convey what I mean. It was more of a roar. It was a blend of delight, expectation, amusement, derision, and exhilaration. Every face was smiling, every mouth open, every eye glistening. As the first hoarse echoes died a sound of gratified mumbling succeeded, as when the lions at the Zoo, having bellowed at the first glimpse of their food, merely pant and lick their lips till the raw meat is flung to them.

Kirkintulloch was waiting for me at the foot of the steps. He looked a trifle shamefaced, I thought, and I fancied I heard him say to a bystander as I went towards him, " Aweel, it's nae business o' mine ! "

Presently it pleased the mob to adopt a facetious tone, and as Kirkintulloch elbowed a passage for me through the crowd, I heard on all sides cries of " Here comes the champion ! " " He's guy jaunty-like ! " " Eh ! but he looks awfy fierce ! " " Gude luck ti ye, ma man ! " " He's a born gowfer ! " " Gude sakes ! He's a braw opeenion o' himsel' ! " " The puir lamb's awa tae the slaughter ! " " It's an ill day this for Jim Lindsay ! " (this with a blatant laugh intended to convey irony). " Ay ! His pride'll hae a fa', nae doot ! " and the like.

XI

AN EXPECTANT CROWD

OF a sudden my heart stood still, and for a moment I stopped dead. There in front of me, and approaching by a series of jinks and dives amid the crowd, was the ghostly figure of the Cardinal. Faint and ill-defined as the apparition seemed in the brilliant sunshine, there was no mistaking the cadaverous features or the flowing robes. In less time than it takes to tell he had reached my side and was whispering into my ear.

" Dinna mind thae folk, " he said, " they'll sing anither tune afore the day's dune. And dinna mind me. I'm no veesible to livin' soul but yerself, and nane but yer ain ears can hear what I'm sayin'. But if ye've a mind tae speak tae me,

a' ye've got tae dae is to *thenk ;* tae speak
in tae yersel, as it were ; for I can thole
the jist o' yer thochts, wi' no sae muckle
as a soond frae yer lips."

I was flabbergasted.

" Sic a clanjamfray o' vermin ! " he
added, as he swept a contemptuous glance
over the noisy mob.

But his presence exasperated me beyond
endurance.   My nerves were strung to all
but the breaking strain, and I found a
relief in venting my spleen on this self-
appointed colleague of mine.

" Look here," I said, and I was at no
pains to conceal my ill-humour, " I'm fed
up with you !   You understand, I'm sick
of you and your devilish wiles.   I'm no
longer in your power, and I snap my
fingers at you.   Get out ! "

I had neglected His Eminence's instructions only to *think* when I addressed him,
and the crowd naturally regarded my words
as a sally in reply to its own ponderous wit.

The result was a babel of words, furious,
jocular, jeering.

"Did ye ever hear the like?" "Ay! Did ye hear him say ' deevilish wiles '? An' this a Presbyterian toon forbye!" "Mercy on us! An' ma man an elder in Doctor MacBide's kirk!" "Awa wi' the bairns; a'll no hae their ears contaaminated," and so on.

"Hoots toots!" was the Cardinal's response, "and you a gentleman! I'm fair ashamed o' ye. But ye canna win awa' frae yer oath, ye ken. It wad mean perdeetion to yer soul an ye did, though I'm far frae assertin' that ye'll no receive that guerdon as it is."

I stopped again, with the intention of arguing out the point once and for all, when I realised that if I went on addressing this invisible spectre, I might possibly be mistaken for a madman. I therefore contented myself with a withering glance of abhorrence at the prelate, and a few unspoken words to the effect that nothing in heaven or earth would induce me to have further truck with him. I then walked calmly on, but I was conscious of

the ghostly presence dogging my steps
with grim persistence, and several times
I heard the never-to-be-forgotten voice
mutter, " Ay ! We'll jist see," or " M'hm !
Is he daft, I wonder ? "

At last I reached the inner circle of the
crowd, and at the teeing ground Lindsay
came forward, looking, I am bound to
admit, the picture of manly health and
vigour.

He held out his hand.

I accepted it with dignity, then looked
about me, bowing here and there as I
recognised acquaintances. This section
of the crowd showed signs of better breeding. There was neither vulgar laughter
nor insolent jeering. On the contrary, its
demeanour was so extremely grave as to
suggest to my sensitive imagination a
suspicion of covert irony. I recognised
many celebrities of the golfing world.
There was Grayson, who wept if he missed
a put, and spent his evenings in chewing
the cud of his daily strokes to the ears of
his depressed but resigned family. There

too was Twinkle, the founder of the Oxbridge Golf Club, whose " style " was as remarkable as his mastery of the technical " language " of the game. Near him was General Simpkins, who, having had a vast experience of fighting on the sandy plains of the Sahara, now employed his old age in exploring the sandy tracts of the St. Magnus bunkers so assiduously that he seldom, if ever, played a stroke on the grass. He was one of the many golfers who find a difficulty in getting up a " foursome." Not far off was Sir William Wilkins, another notable enthusiast, whose scores when playing alone are remarkably low, though he seldom does a hole in less than eight strokes if playing in a game or under the scrutiny of a casual onlooker. I nodded to Mr. Henry Grove, the celebrated actor-manager, and a keen golfer. I didn't know that he was celebrated when first I met him, but I gathered it from the few minutes' conversation that passed between us.

Standing near the Lowchesters was Mrs.

Gunter, in a heavenly confection of shell-pink and daffodil-yellow, a sort of holiday frock, delicate in tint, and diaphanous as a sufficiently modest spider's web. She greeted me with the brightest of smiles, and laughingly kissed her finger-tips to me. Certainly she was the most charming woman present. Her bright colour and gleaming hair seemed to defy the wind and sunshine, though I fancy that rain might have proved a trifle inconvenient. There was no manner of doubt that I loved her. She represented to me a sort of allegorical figurehead symbolising affluence, luxury, and independence. That is, assuming that she would consent to occupy the central niche in my own ambitious temple of matrimony.

Even the University of St. Magnus was represented in the gathering by a group of its professors, rusty-looking gentlemen who betrayed no indication of anything so trivial as a bygone youth ; but, on the contrary, closely resembled a number of chief mourners at the funeral of their own

intellects. A notable figure was the genial
and cultured Doctor MacBide, one of the
ablest and most popular divines that
Scotland has given to the world, one in
whom is to be found the rare combination
of an æsthetic soul allied to a fearless
character, a man who, keeping one eye on
heaven and the other on earth, has used
both to the benefit of the world in general
and St. Magnus in particular.

Mr. Monktown, the more or less dis-
tinguished politician, was also in the
crowd. His eyes had the far-away look
of a minor celebrity on whom has been
forced the conviction that due recognition
of his talents will never be found this side
of the grave. On the other hand, his
charming and brilliant wife conveys the
impression that she will continue to lustily
insist on the aforesaid recognition until a
peerage or some such badge of notoriety
is administered as a narcotic by a peace-at-
any-price premier.

But to enumerate all the interesting
people in the dense crowd is an impossible

task. Suffice it to say that such a con-
stellation of golfing stars could be seen
only on the links of St. Magnus, with
perhaps the single exception of those of
St. Andrews.

How little did the crowd guess that,
unruffled and confident as I seemed, I yet
knew that I was destined to a humiliating
defeat ; and how much less did I know
what a bitter thing is defeat to a man
of my sanguine temperament and former
achievements !

XII

THE MATCH BEGINS

I WAS startled from a brief brown study by the sound of Lindsay's voice.

" Shall we toss for the honour ? "

" As you please," I replied.

He spun a coin.

" Head or tail ? "

I chose the head.

" It's a tail," he said, as, pocketing the coin, he took the driver that his caddie handed.

Then he drove. It was a magnificent shot, straight and sure, and the ball landed half-way between the public road and the stream that bounds the first putting green. A murmur of approval rose from the crowd.

Then I took up position.

Again a murmur arose from the crowd, but not a reassuring one.

Kirkintulloch endeavoured to inspire me with confidence as he handed me my driver by whispering in a hoarse, spirituous undertone that must have been audible to everyone near, " Dinna mind the crowd, sir. Just pretend that ye *caan* goalf."

I was about to address the ball when my eye caught sight of the Cardinal. His face was livid with rage, and I could barely repress a chuckle as he shrieked in a voice that apparently only reached my ears (for the crowd never budged), " Tak' the auld clubs, I tell 'ee ! "

Afraid of betraying myself by vacant look or startled mien, I ignored His Eminence's fury, and precipitately drove the ball.

I topped it.

It shot along the ground, hurling itself against casual stones, as if under the impression that I was a billiard player desirous of making a break in cannons.

Then we moved on.

As we walked over the hundred yards that my ball had travelled, the Cardinal sidled up to me, and thrusting his face (through which I could clearly see a view of beach and sea) close to mine, exclaimed, " Ye're a fule ! "

I took no notice. I was beginning to enjoy the discomfiture of one who had caused me such acute sufferings a few hours before.

" D'ye hear ? " he persisted. " Wi' yer ain clubs ye're no match for a callant like Lindsay ! For ony sake, tak' mine. Are ye feared the folk'll laugh at sic ante-diluvian implements? Ye needna mind the mob, I assure ye. If ye win hole after hole, ye'll turn the laugh on Lindsay, nae maitter what the clubs be like. Forbye, there's yer oath."

I still ignored him, and I saw the yellow teeth grind in silent fury.

Meantime, behind us plodded the crowd, the dull thud of their steps on the spongy grass almost drowned by their voluble and exasperating chatter.

There are no words in my vocabulary to express the humiliation that I felt as I played. I was at my worst. My second shot landed me about a hundred yards further ; Lindsay dropped his on to the putting green. With my third the ball travelled to the burn and stopped there, embedding itself in the soft black mud. This incident afforded unbounded delight to the mob, and I fancied that I heard Mrs. Gunter's silvery laugh. The only satisfaction that I experienced was in the uncontrollable rage of the Cardinal. He danced and leapt about me, gesticulating wildly, alternately pouring sixteenth-century vituperation into my ears, and imploring me to use his accursed clubs. He even indulged in weeping on the off-chance of softening my heart, but I saw no pathos in the tears that flowed down his spectral cheek from eyes that never lost their vindictive glare.

Lindsay behaved extremely well. He showed no sign of triumph as he won hole after hole, and several times he turned upon the crowd and upbraided them roundly for the howls of laughter with which they received my miserable efforts. Kirkintulloch became gradually more and more depressed, and eventually took the line of a Job's comforter.

" It's jist as I tell't ye. He's layin' ye oot like a corp," said he.

" Well, let him," I growled.

" It's mesel' I'm thinkin' o'. Ye see I've a poseetion tae keep up. They a' ken I've been learnin' ye the game, forbye I'm the professional champion. I'll be fair howled at when I gang in tae the public-hoose the nicht."

" Then the simple remedy is not to go there," I argued.

" Whaat ? No gang tae the public-hoose ? "

I had apparently propounded a quite unheard-of course of action, but I stuck to it, and said, " No."

" Aweel," he resumed, " a' I can say is ye dinna ken oor faimily " (which was true). " Ma faither never missed a nicht

but what he was half-seas over in the
' Gowfer's Arms,' an' it's no in my blood to
forget the words, ' Honour yer faither and
mither,' an' a' the rest o' it. So I just dae
the same, and it's a grand tribute to the
memory o' my kith and kin. Forbye—I
like it. I canna sleep if I'm ower sober."

I leave the reader to imagine my feelings
as Kirkintulloch thus unfolded the heredi-
tary tendencies of his family to one ear,
and the Cardinal poured violent anathemas
into the other. The crowd was convulsed
in spasms of derisive delight at each of my
futile strokes, and certainly Mrs. Gunter
seemed furtively amused when I ventured
to glance in her direction. Only Wetherby
was unmoved. Bearing the Cardinal's
clubs, he followed me at a discreet distance, with an inscrutable expression that
would have done credit to a priest of the
Delphic Oracle.

I got into every possible bunker, to the
noisy gratification of the mob which,
despite the frequent remonstrances of the
better class of people present, had now

abandoned itself to the wildest hilarity. The match was, in fact, a harlequinade, with Lindsay as the clever clown and myself as the idiotic pantaloon.

I seemed to tread on air, with only a vague idea of what was going on.

By a lucky fluke I won the short hole, albeit in a rather undignified manner. Mr. Lindsay's caddie, though some distance off, was nevertheless slightly in front of me as I drove, and my ball (which I topped so that it shot away at right angles) struck his boot, on which Kirkintulloch loudly claimed the hole.

At the " turn " (*i.e.* the end of the first nine holes) I was seven down ; and at the end of the eighteen—let me confess it at once—Lindsay was sixteen up.

The first round over, the garrulous crowd dispersed in various directions, gabbling, cackling, laughing, and howling with an absence of breeding truly astounding.

Even the " society " section no longer concealed its amusement. I have never understood the limitations of that word

" society." It seems to me such an elastic term nowadays, that if a person says he is in it, then *ipso facto* he is. Formerly it applied exclusively to my own class, *i.e.* the aristocracy ; but since we latter have taken to emulating the peculiarities and tendencies of the criminal classes we are possibly excluded.

An interval of an hour and a half was allowed for luncheon, and it was arranged that we should meet for the final round at 2.30 p.m.

I refused all invitations to lunch at the club or at private houses, and retired to a solitary meal in my own room.

But it was only solitary in a sense.

I had just begun to tackle a mutton cutlet and tomato sauce when, raising my eyes for a moment to look for the salt, I beheld my ubiquitous Cardinal seated opposite me.

This was a little too much, and seizing a decanter of claret I hurled it in his face. His shadowy features offered so little re-sistance that the wine eventually distributed itself over Wetherby, who seemed for once mildly surprised.

I muttered an apology to that irreproachable domestic, explaining that the liquor was corked, and then I desired him to leave the room.

I was alone with my tormentor, and I determined to have it out with him. But His Eminence anticipated me, for whilst I was framing in my mind a declamatory and indignant exordium, he leaned across the table, and with a singularly suave voice and subdued manner addressed me as follows :—

" I apologise, young sir, if I have caused you ony inconvenience on this momentous occasion. I was ower keen, an' I tak a' the blame o' yer ill fortune on ma ain shoulders. Just eat your denner like a man, and dinna fash yersel' wi' me ; but when ye've feenished, an ye'll be sae gude as to hear me for the space of five meenits, I'll be obleeged. Mair than that, I'll undertake that ye'll no' be worrit by me again."

This was an important offer, and a certain unexpected charm in my unbidden guest's suavity turned the balance in his favour.

"Do you mean," I asked, "that if I grant you a short interview when I have finished luncheon, you will undertake to cease annoying me by your enervating companionship and intemperate language?"

"That's it," replied the prelate.

"Very good," said I ; "I agree."

I continued the meal. Wetherby returned with a fresh bottle of wine and a custard pudding, brought me cigarettes, coffee, and Cognac in due course, and though in the discharge of his duties he frequently walked through the dim anatomy of my ecclesiastical patron, his doing so seemed to afford no inconvenience whatever to that perplexing prelate.

As I ate and drank in silence my red-robed friend paced the room with bent head and thoughful mien, in the manner adopted by every Richelieu that I have seen on the stage. I fancied that I detected a wistful glance in his eyes as from time to time I raised a glass of wine to my lips, but I may have been mistaken.

It must seem odd to the matter-of-fact reader that I could golf, talk, eat, drink, and generally comport myself as an ordinary mortal whilst haunted by this remarkable spectre; but the fact is, I had no choice in the matter. Suppose I had drawn the attention of my neighbours to the fact that I was pursued by a shadowy Cardinal! It was abundantly clear that none but I could see him, and I should only have been laughed at. And, after all, a man of my varied experiences and quick intelligence adapts himself, through sheer force of habit, to any situation, though at the time he may utterly fail to comprehend its *raison d'être* or significance.

At one period of the meal I was on the point of asking Wetherby if he saw no faintly defined figure, robed in red and standing near him. But just as I was about to speak to him he advanced with the coffee, and in setting down the tray actually stood within the same cubic space that the Cardinal occupied. That is to say, I distinctly saw them mixed up with each other, Wetherby passing in and out of the prelate's robes quite unconsciously. Nor did His Eminence seem to mind, for not only did the coffee and Cognac pass through the region of his stomach, but also the tray, cups, saucers, and cigarettes.

XIII

I TEST THE CLUBS

M Y luncheon over, I pushed back the plates, drank a glass of Cognac, poured out a cup of coffee, and lit a cigarette.

The combined effects of the fresh air of

the links and the moderately good wine I had drunk during lunch had braced me up, and as the first puff of pale blue smoke left my lips, I leaned back in my

"WELL, OLD MAN, OUT WITH IT!"

chair and contemplated my guest. " Well, old man," said I, with perhaps undue familiarity, " out with it ! "

He turned and swept me such a graceful bow that I felt a sheepish shame at the flippant and vulgar tone I had adopted.

" I will noo mak' ye a final proposal, young sir," he said. " Ahint the hotel is a secluded field, and if ye'll tak' ma clubs there and try a shot or two, I ask nae mair. If so be ye find a speecial virtue in them, gude and weel ; if no', then a' thing is ower atween us, and the even tenour o' yer way'll no be interfered wi' by me."

I saw what he meant. I was to try the clubs and test the marvellous qualities that he insisted on.

Well, there was no harm in that.

I rang the bell, and told Wetherby to carry the clubs to the field indicated by my ghostly counsellor.

It was a good grass meadow of some ten acres, and not a soul was near, with, of course, the exception of the Cardinal.

I teed a ball, and selecting a club that most resembled a driver (though it was more like a gigantic putter than anything else), I began to address the ball.

As I did so I experienced a curious sensation.

I suddenly felt as if I had been a golfer all my life. There was no longer any hesitation as to where my hands or feet should be. Instinctively I fell into the right attitude.

I was no longer self-conscious. I found myself addressing the ball with the same easy grace I had observed in Kirkintulloch. A sense of extraordinary power came over me. My legs and arms tingled as if some strong stimulant were flowing in my veins. The club had taken a mastery over me. I swung it almost involuntarily, and the first shot was by far the finest drive I had ever made. I tried again and yet again, six shots in all, and each was as straight and sure as the very best of Lindsay's.

I was amazed and dumbfounded.

" Weel ! Did I no' tell ye ? " cried the Cardinal, as he hopped about in a grotesque and undignified ecstasy. " Try the putter noo ! "

I took the putter. It was something like a flat-headed croquet mallet, and very heavy. Then I threw a silver matchbox on the ground to represent a hole, and began to put.

I simply couldn't miss it. A sense of awe came over me.

No matter from what distance I played, nor how rough the ground was, the ball went straight to the box, as a needle to a magnet. I even tried to miss it and failed in the attempt.

I looked at His Eminence, and words fail me to describe the childish yet passionate exultation that shone in his face.

" I can dae nae mair ! " he cried. " Ye see what they're like. Play wi' them, and ye'll win as sure as my name's Alexander Smeaton ! It's a fact. Ay ! And ye've time to wander into the club-hoose and lay yer wagers, if ye're minded to mak' a

wheen siller. For the love o' ma auld
bones, dae as I tell ye, man!"

I didn't at all love his old bones, but my
mind was made up.

"I'll play with the clubs," I said, and
the old man staggered in an intensity of
delight.

"Hech! sir," he cried, "this'll be a
grand day for Sandy Smeaton! When
the match is ower I'll be there to compliment ye, and then—aweel, then I'll no fash
ye till ye 'shuffle off yer mortal coil,' as
auld Bacon has it. When ye're like myself—a speerit, ye ken—ye may be glad
tae hae a freend at court, an' I'll dae what
I can for ye. I can introduce ye to a'
the canonised saints. They're a wheen
ponderous in conversation and awfy or-
thodox in doctrine, but on the whole
verra respectable. Hooever, that'll no'
be for a while. Meantime, young sir, win
yer match and humeeliate this varmint
spawn o' the hoose o' Lindsay. So—
'Buon giorno'—as we used to say in the
auld Vatican days—'A rivederci!'"

With these valedictory remarks the Cardinal left me, and returning the clubs to Wetherby, who had been standing some hundred yards off, I returned to the hotel.

It was two o'clock.

How shall I describe what I felt? I could win this match—of that I felt absolutely sure. I cannot explain this curious sense of certainty as to the issue of the game, but I knew by a sort of prophetic inspiration that I could not lose.

The Cardinal had hinted at wagers. Well, why not?

I could turn the tables on some of the crowd who had smiled in pity at my efforts of the morning, and there is no revenge so sweet as that of scoring off men who have laughed at one. I decided to get a little money on the event, if possible.

I strolled leisurely over to the club and entered the smoking-room, an immense room with bay windows that open on to the links. It was crowded. The members had finished luncheon, and were discussing coffee, liqueurs, cigars, and cigarettes, amid a noisy jingle of laughter, talk, clinking of glasses, tinkling of cups, hurrying footsteps of waiters, and general hubbub.

My entrance had something of the effect that oil has on troubled waters. Everybody near me ceased laughing. No doubt I had been the bull's-eye for their hilarious shafts of wit. They hummed and hawed as if I had detected them in some nefarious plot. A few bowed to me, and one or two invited me to have a drink. But I was bent on business, so, joining a group in which I saw a few acquaintances, I asked casually if any bets had been made on the match.

" Not one, don't you know ! " replied O'Hagan, a Scotch youth of Irish name, who cultivated a highly ornate English accent with intermittent success.

" Anybody want a bet ? " I asked, adding, " Of course I should want very heavy odds."

There was a general movement on this. Members gathered round me, some laughing, some chaffing, some whispering. Lowchester came up to me, and growled in an undertone, " Don't make a fool of yourself, my dear chap ; you can't possibly win."

" Still, I don't mind making a bet or two," I persisted. " Will anyone lay me fifty to one ? "

" I'll lay you forty to one in fivers," said Mr. Grove, the actor, no doubt considering the publicity of the offer as a good advertisement.

" Done ! " I replied, and took a note of it.

" So will I ! " " And I ! " " Put me down for the same." " In sovereigns ? " " Yes." " Tenners if you like ! " " Done ! "

These and other cries now sounded all round the room till the babel reminded me of the Stock Exchange, and I think quite two-thirds of the men present laid me the odds at forty to one in sovereigns, fivers, or tenners.

I suppose they considered me a madman, or at least an intolerably vain and eccentric person who deserved a " dressing down." A hurried adding up of my bets showed me that I stood to lose about £250, or win £10,000.

It was now close on two o'clock, and we moved off to the links. The crowd was not quite so dense. Evidently many people considered the match as good as over, and the interest of those who remained was almost apathetic. The heavy midday meal that is eaten in St. Magnus may account to some extent for this lethargy.

I found the faithful Wetherby waiting for me, at a discreetly remote distance, and telling him that I meant to play with the clubs he was carrying, I walked up to Kirkintulloch. The latter had all the air of a martyr. His head was thrown back, as if in the act of challenging the world in general to laugh at him. He glared suspiciously at everyone near him, and with difficulty brought himself to touch his hat at my approach.

I chuckled inwardly.

" Whaat's this I hear, sir ? " he said. " Ye've been wagerin', they tell me."

" I've made a few bets, if that's what you mean," I answered.

" Weel, sir, as man tae man, if ye'll excuse the leeberty, ye're fair demented. It's no' possible to win. A'body kens that. As for mesel', I'm the laughin'-stock o' the toon. I huvna had sae muckle as time for ma denner——"

" Why not ? " I asked.

" I've been busy blackin' the een and spleetin' the nebs o' yer traducers. I've been fechtin' seeven men. It's a caddie's beesiness to stand up for his maister, nae maitter what kind o' a gowfer he is."

" Ah, well ! " I answered, " you'll make them sing to another tune to-night. I am going to play with these."

And uncovering the canvas flap that concealed them, I exposed the weird-looking clubs to his gaze.

I think he thought I was joking. He looked first at the clubs, and then at me, with a half-questioning, half-stupid twinkle in his hard, blue eyes. Then he spat.

I apologise to the reader for mentioning anything so unpleasant, but it is an uncomfortable habit that certain classes indulge in when they desire to punctuate or emphasise their views. Amongst themselves, I believe, it is considered highly expressive, if employed at the true psychological moment.

" What kin' o' things are they ? " he asked, after a portentous pause.

" The clubs I mean to play with," I replied.

" Aweel ! " he answered, " that concludes a' relations atween us. I may be daft, but I'm no' a fule, an' I'm seek of the hale stramash. Ye mun get another caddie, I'll no cairry the likes o' thae things."

" My servant is going to carry them," I answered quickly ; and I fancied Kirkintulloch looked a trifle crestfallen at such an unexpected exhibition of independence.

" I'll be glad, however," I added, " if you'll accompany me round the links, and

I promise you the pleasing sensation of astonishment if you do."

With this I left him, but I could hear fragments of a voluble explanation that he apparently deemed it necessary to make to the bystanders.

" There are leemits, ye ken—it's no' for the likes o' me to say—I've been a caddie twenty-fower year—the man's no' richt in the heed—no' but what he's free with his siller an' a born gentleman—I wouldna say he wasna—but ma name's Kirkintulloch, an' I've a poseetion tae keep up."

The clock of the parish church boomed out the half-hour, and I advanced to the teeing ground, with Wetherby at my heels. The flap had been replaced over the heads of the clubs, and the bag looked ordinary enough, though my new " caddie " was so faultlessly attired in his well-cut grey suit as to be a target for the derision of a number of Kirkintulloch's professional friends.

XIV

THE SECOND ROUND

THE " honour " being Lindsay's, the
first drive was his. It was a clean-
hit ball, but a wind had arisen that carried
it a trifle out of the course.

Then I took my stand, and received
from Wetherby the Cardinal's driver.

Of all hearty laughter that my ears have
ever listened to, none could equal that of
the bystanders who were near enough to
see the club. If I had made the most
witty joke that mind can conceive, it
could not have elicited more spontaneous,
prolonged, or uproarious appreciation.
Mrs. Gunter's mezzo-soprano rang out in
a paroxysm of musical hysterics. Even
Lindsay edged behind me that I might
not see the smile he found it impossible

to repress. Members of the club and
their friends, who had behaved with de-
corous gravity during the morning, now
abandoned themselves frankly to unre-
strained laughter. The infection spread
to the masses of the crowd who were not
near enough to see my curious club, and
they gradually pressed closer and closer,
anxious to share and enjoy any new source
of merriment, so that it took the men with
the rope all their time to maintain the
semicircle that divided the spectators from
the players.

Under ordinary circumstances I should
have resented such behaviour, but somehow it didn't seem to affect me. I even
felt inclined to join in the general hilarity.
I certainly felt the humour of the situation.
As it was, I approached the ball with
perfect composure and the ghost of a
sardonic smile.

And then I drove it.

Away it winged, hard-hit and fast,
travelling straight in the line of the hole.
I had never, of course, played such a

magnificent shot, and the effect on the crowd was electrical. Laughter died of a sudden, as if choked in a thousand throats. Broad grins seemed frozen on the upraised faces round me. Mouths opened unconsciously, eyes stared vacantly at the flying ball. For the moment I was surrounded by so many living statues, transfixed in mute amazement.

I think it was Lowchester who first spoke. " A fine shot," I fancied I heard him say mechanically.

We moved on, and the act of walking loosened the tongues around me. A confused murmuring ensued, gradually increasing in volume till everybody seemed to be talking and arguing, agreeing with or contradicting each other at the pitch of the voice.

I caught stray phrases from time to time. " I never seed the likes o' that." " Man, it was a braw drive ! " " He'll no' dae it again, I'm thinkin'." " By Jove ! that was a flyer—but what an extraordinary club ! " and so on.

I had outdriven Lindsay by about sixty yards—no small feat when one bears in mind that he has the reputation of being the longest driver living.

His second shot was a good one, landing him some thirty yards short of the burn. As we reached my ball, I selected the Cardinal's ponderous and much-corroded cleek. There were faint indications of amusement at the sight of it, but a nervous curiosity as to my next shot was the predominating note.

I played the shot quite easily. As before, the ball flew straight as a bird in the line of the hole, crossed the burn and dropped dead within a few feet of the flag. An unwilling murmur of admiration rose from the crowd, and Lindsay, no longer smiling, said very frankly that he had never seen two finer strokes in his life.

I think it only right to admit that he is a sensible, manly, and modest fellow.

He took his lofting iron and with a very neat wrist shot dropped the ball dead, within a foot of the hole.

A hearty cheer greeted the stroke. It was quite evident that he was the popular favourite. Well, I could wait, and I meant to.

Arrived on the putting-green, I advanced with the odd-looking putter. One or two of the spectators indulged in a cynical, though somewhat half-hearted, snigger at its curious lines, but for the most part the crowd was quite silent, and one could almost feel in the air the nervous tension of the onlookers. My ball was about seven feet from the hole. With complete self-possession I went up to it and glanced almost carelessly at the ground.

There was a dead silence.

I played, and the ball dropped lightly into the hole. I was one up on the second round. I had holed out in three.

I half expected a murmur of applause for the put, but a bewildered stupor was the actual effect produced. In all that concourse of people only two appeared to be quite calm and collected, namely, Wetherby and myself. I caught a glimpse of Kirkintulloch's face. The features were there, but all expression had departed.

For myself, I walked on air. The outward calm of my demeanour gave no index to the wild exultation that I felt. Truly there is no more satisfying or stimulating anticipation than that of a coming revenge. The sentiment, I am aware, is not a Christian one, but at least it is eminently human. I felt no desire to be revenged on Lindsay. Any hostile feeling that I had entertained towards him had passed away. But I did desire to score off the crowd. More, I desired to humiliate Mrs. Gunter. Her callous treatment of me, her silvery but malicious laughter, her avowed admiration of Lindsay, had galled me to an extent the expression of which I have carefully kept from these pages. *Noblesse oblige!* One cannot be rude. But I wanted to annoy her—a very common phase of love.

As the match proceeded I won hole after hole, often in the most astonishing manner. Twice I landed in bunkers close to the greens (the result of exceptionally long shots), and in each case the Cardinal's iron lifted the ball from the sand and deposited it in the hole. I cannot take credit to myself for such prodigious feats ; they were undoubtedly the work of the clubs.

At the eighth hole, however, I experienced an important reverse. It is, as everybody who knows the St. Magnus links is aware, the short hole. I took the iron and dropped the ball within a yard of the hole. Lindsay followed, and landed some twenty yards off ; and then, by a splendid put, he holed out in two. I, of course, had no difficulty in doing likewise, and we halved the hole ; but the awkward fact remained that I must now gain every hole to win the match, for my opponent's score was " nine up," and there only remained ten holes to play.

If the match was intensely exciting—and to me it was more than that—the demeanour of the crowd was no less psychologically interesting. The tag-rag and bobtail, with the fickleness that has ever

characterised the emotions of the un-
washed, and even of the occasionally
clean, now began to acclaim me as their
chosen champion, and each brilliant shot
I made was hailed with a vociferous delight that might have turned a less steadily
balanced head than my own. The reason
of this is, of course, more or less obvious.
There is more pleasurable excitement to
be derived from making a god of the man
whose star is in the ascendant than in con-
tinuing allegiance with falling crest to one
whom we have placed on a pinnacle by an
error of judgment, to which we are loath
to attract attention.

But if the crowd was a source of ever-
increasing interest, what shall I say of the
demeanour of the men who had made
heavy bets with me ?

It is not strictly true that Scotchmen are
mean in money matters, any more than it
is to say that they can't see a joke. As
regards the latter point, it is my experience
that a Scot won't laugh at the average
jest that amuses an Englishman, simply

because it isn't good enough.   And since he doesn't laugh he is supposed to have missed the point.   In support of my theory is the fact that there is an established vein of Scotch wit and humour, but I have yet to learn that England has evolved any-thing of the sort.   True, England has many comic papers, and Scotland has none.   But it must be borne in mind that the statements announcing such periodi-cals to be " comic " emanate solely from the proprietors.

There is, however, a substratum—or rather a perversion—of truth in the aphor-ism that deals with the Scotch and their money.   And I take it the real truth is that a Scot cannot bear to part with money for which he gets no return of any sort—a very natural and proper feeling.   Again, he dislikes any extra or unusual call on his purse.   For the rest he is generous, hospitable, and public-spirited to a degree. It may be argued that if this be the case the Scot ought never to make a bet ; the answer to which is that as a rule he doesn't, unless something almost in the nature of a certainty presents itself. Then he forgets his nationality and becomes merely human. And that is precisely what happened to my Caledonian friends in the smoking-room of the club. An apparently unprecedented opportunity of making a little money had presented itself, and they had accepted its conditions with a noisy humour intended to lacquer their inbred acquisitive propensities.

And now, as I casually watched their faces, I saw an interesting awakening. Their faces were as those of infants who, having been roused from a long and profound sleep, gaze about with inquiring but stupefied wonder. They were quite silent for the most part, as with every shot I played they seemed to feel the sovereigns melting in their pockets. Ah! this unhappy craze for gold! I have seen the same set faces at Monte Carlo, when, as the croupier cries out, " Rouge, Pair et Passe ! " the bulk of the money is staked on " Noir, Impair et Manque." How deplorable it all is! And I stood to win £10,000—a most exhilarating prospect.

XV

IN THE THROES

A S the match progressed I continued
playing an absolutely faultless game,
and there was no manner of doubt that
Lindsay had become more or less demoralised. At the end of the fifteenth
hole his score was reduced to two up,
with three more holes to play. That is
to say, so far I had won every hole of the
second round, with the exception of the
short one which we had halved. I had
only to win the last three holes to gain
the match, nay more, to break the record
score of the links !

A curious change in the crowd's bearing
was now apparent. They preserved a
complete silence. Each shot, whether
my own or Lindsay's, was played in a

profound stillness. An intense suppressed excitement seemed to consume every soul present. Even during the marches from shot to shot scarcely a word was spoken ; only the dull thud of thousands of feet gave audible token of their presence.

The news of the sudden and extraordinary change in the fortunes of the game had evidently travelled backwards to St. Magnus, for as we worked homewards the mob was increased at every hole by such vast numbers that it seemed impossible for the men with the rope to control so great a concourse.

Once or twice I glanced in Mrs. Gunter's direction, and I should have thought her face was pale but for two vivid splashes of a most exquisite carmine that glowed, or at all events dwelt, on her cheeks. Her jet-black eyebrows formed two thoughtful lines below the golden cloud of her beautiful hair. How resplendent she was! I have never seen a complexion at all like hers except on the stage. What wonder that Lindsay should be demoralised, with the prospect of being forestalled hanging over him like the sword of Damocles?

Only once did I catch sight of the shadowy Cardinal, and that was at the end of the sixteenth hole, which I had won easily. As we walked towards the teeing ground of the seventeenth I chanced to let my eyes fall on the railway shed built against the wall bounding the links, and there—executing the most extraordinary and grotesque fandango of delight—was His Eminence. He was evidently in a rapture of delirious intoxication, for, in the passing glimpse I had, I saw him standing on his head, so that the ghostly robes fell downward to the roof of the shed, leaving his white skeleton immodestly bare and feet upwards in the air. It was not a pleasing exhibition, and very nearly unnerved me ; but the mere handling of my marvellous driver seemed to steady me in a moment. And fortunately none but I could see the antics of my ecclesiastical patron.

Reader, do you know what it is to be

"EXECUTING THE MOST EXTRAORDINARY FANDANGO
OF DELIGHT "

outwardly as calm as a *blasé* policeman, and all the time quivering with inward excitement ? If I could have yelled once or twice it would have been an immense relief, but I had a part to play, and I meant to play it. As it was, I puffed carelessly at a cigarette, professed to admire the view, glanced carelessly at my watch, and generally indulged in such little bits of by-play as were calculated to indicate extreme *sang-froid*. [I ought to mention that I am a very capable amateur actor, and at our annual Thespian Club theatricals always take the leading part. I founded the club and manage it.]

That I played my new rôle of champion golfer with credit was evident. The seething crowd had originally assembled to jeer, but it remained to accept me at my own valuation—always a pleasing change to find registered in the barometer of public opinion.

My drive at the seventeenth hole (the last but one to be played) was a perfect shot, whilst Lindsay's was comparatively feeble. He was now but one up, and at the end of the hole we ought to be " all square and one to play." But the strain on my nerves was beginning to tell. I felt like Hood's Eugene Aram—

> " Merrily rose the lark, and shook
>   The dewdrop from its wing ;
> But I never marked its morning flight,
>   I never heard it sing ;
> For I was stooping once again
>   Beneath the horrid thing ! "

I was conscious in a vague somnambulistic fashion of the green links, the blue sky, the purple crowd, splashed here and there with the bright colours of frock and parasol. My eyes took in mechanically the onward movement of the people, the rosy light that caught the spires of the old grey town, the shrieking railway train, the red blaze of the sun in the windows of St. Magnus, and a hundred other ocular impressions. Yet all these things seemed unreal ; the dream background in a land whereof the Cardinal, Lindsay, and I formed the sole population.

Moreover, pressing as it seemed on my very brain, came the humiliating conviction that I was nothing short of a fraud, a charlatan, a ghostly conjurer's accomplice.

Was it an honourable game that I was playing ? Would I be justified in taking the money I stood to win ? Was it fair to usurp the throne of champion by the aid of a supernatural agency, whose purpose I could not even pretend to fathom ? Could I look Mrs. Gunter in the face if, crowned with a stolen golfing halo, I asked her to be my wife ? And if I couldn't, what more deplorable type of lover was possible ? Ought I to burden myself with a secret that I should have to carry with me in silence to the grave ? Was the nominal prefix " Honourable," with which my parents had dowered me without either warrant on my part or inquiry on their own, to be a prefix only ? These and many other thoughts flashed through my mind as we played the seventeenth hole.

I got on the green in three, Lindsay in four. He then played the " two more," and by a remarkably good put holed out in five.

I took the putter, and in a profound and most impressive silence holed out in four. A stifled gasp rose from the crowd.

The score was now, " All square, and one to play."

I stood on the teeing ground of the eighteenth hole. The landscape in front of me was blurred and blotted ; the dense crowds on either side of me were as mere inky blotches. The ground at my feet seemed miles away. Only the teed ball was in focus. That I saw clearly.

It was a test moment in my life. I could lose the match if I chose, and keep a clean conscience.

I could play the last hole with my own clubs !

And if I did—well, I'd lose ; but, by Heaven ! I'd still be an honourable gentleman.

I caught sight of Lindsay's face. It was white and set, but he looked a manly fellow for all that. It was a cowardly trick to tear the laurels from his brow as I was doing. He had won them after a lifetime's devotion to the game.

And I——?

Faugh! I would not touch the accursed clubs again. For aught I knew, to win was to sell my soul, and become a servile creature doomed to the tender mercies of a phantom's patronage.

*　　*　　*　　*　　*

"Ye fushiomless eediot!" I suddenly heard the words ring in my ears, and at the same moment I saw the Cardinal's deadly face peering into my eyes as if to read my very soul. "What's come ower ye? Are ye daft? Nane o' yer pauky humour at this time o' day. Tak' ma driver an' catch the ba' the bonniest skite of a'! Whaat?"—and his voice rose in indescribable fury—"Ye'll no do sic a thing? Ye lily-livered loon, if ye dinna dae as I tell ye I'll hae ye back in the castle vaults and wring the neck o' yer soul wi' ma ain bony fingers! Ay, an'

haunt ye till the day ye're deid ! " (What
good purpose could be served by haunting
me till the day of death, after wringing the
neck of my soul, was not quite clear.)
" Mind that ! " he continued, " I'm no' to
be trifled wi' ! "

I turned on him and answered de-
liberately, " You fiend ! "

" Beg pardon, sir ? " said Wetherby.   I
had forgotten for the moment, and spoken
aloud.

" Give me the driver from Kirkintulloch's
bag," I replied.

Kirkintulloch heard me, and elbowed
his way to my side.   He was shaking with
excitement.   I feel certain he had never
been so sober for years.

" Will 'ee no jist gang on wi' the one
ye've been playin' wi' ? " he urged.   " Ye're
daein' fine ! "

" Give me the driver with which I played
the first round this morning," I persisted.

During all this the Cardinal was moving
and shrieking round me in a whirlwind of
red draperies and white corroded bones.

Reluctantly Kirkintulloch drew the driver from his bag, and handed it to me.

" I think ye're wrong, sir," he whispered very earnestly in my ear, mixing himself up with the demented prelate in doing so.

" For Heaven's sake let no one speak to me ! " I cried. " Get out of my way ! " I added fiercely—really to the Cardinal, though Kirkintulloch, Wetherby, and everyone near seemed to take it to themselves, and drew back hastily. Then I gave a vicious kick at His Eminence's shins. Lowchester has since told me the action appeared most inexplicable and uncalled for, inasmuch as I apparently kicked at space.

I addressed the ball.

His Eminence promptly sat on it. Then, stretching his arms in front of me, he cursed me wildly and volubly in Latin. What the exact words were I cannot tell, and could not have translated had I known, but the general effect was awful.

Crash through his bones—not that such

a trifle could inconvenience my intangible enemy—went the club.

The ball, feebly struck on the top, shot along the grass, and dropped into the burn!

The match was as good as lost.

A shriek, whether of delight, dismay, relief, or anxiety, I know not, rose from the mob. I believe everyone in that crowd was suffering from the same nervous strain that affected me.

Then Lindsay stepped to the front.

He drove a magnificent ball, and, strange as it may seem, the mere sight wrought a complete upheaval of the altruistic pedestal on which I had perched myself. I was suddenly conscious of a wild exasperation at having thrown my chances to the winds. For, after all, my objections to winning had been purely sentimental, not to say childish. It is marvellous how the realisation of our best intentions very frequently betrays the insincerity of the moral mood that inspired them. It is easy to be magnanimous if we don't foresee the unhappy but common result of poignant regret.

The vision of a heavenly and luxurious life with Mrs. Gunter seemed to fade. I turned and looked at her. She was as white as a sheet, save for the faithful discs of carmine. Ah, what a fool I had been!

But the game was not yet over; and even as the thought flashed across me, Lindsay made his first serious mistake. It was a mistake of judgment.

" Thank Heaven," he exclaimed, with an ill-bred grunt of relief, " I've cooked your goose for you at last!"

I have no doubt this thoughtless and ill-timed speech was the result of the strain he had been put to. Perhaps I ought to have made allowance for it. In point of fact, it reawakened in me the most consuming desire to win, and I cursed my extravagant magnanimity.

Meantime a rapt and beautiful change had come over the faces of the men with whom I had made bets. Frowns were dissipated as by a ray of beatific sunshine, and lively smiles and chuckles were the order of the moment. There was even a touch of insolence in their sidelong glances. They began to chatter volubly. I could hear the drift of their sudden recall to speech.

" I knew he was bound to break down in the long run," said somebody.

" Undoubtedly ; still he's played a remarkable game." " I win ten pounds "— " and I a fiver," and so forth. My miserable drive had acted on their tongues as the first round of champagne does at dinner.

We were walking towards the burn as Lindsay spoke, and I was about to answer when—springing apparently from nowhere —the Cardinal again appeared, or rather shot up before me, in a state of incontinent frenzy. None the less, he seemed to divine the thoughts that were chasing each other through my mind, for, bending towards me, he whispered in hoarse, trembling tones, and with the utmost intensity—

" Tak' ma club !   Tak' ma club ! !   Tak'

ma club—ye eediot ! ! ! He's dealt ye a black affront ; but, by a' the buried bones o' the Smeatons he hasna yet won the day ! "

" You think I still may win ? " I silently asked him, albeit in a state of incredulous stupefaction.

" Try, man—try ! " he shrieked in reply " I'll see what I can dae ! "

And with that he caught up his skirts and flew off in a series of amazing leaps and bounds in the direction of the last hole. What this change in his tactics meant I was at a loss to conjecture.

I wish I could adequately describe the extraordinary flight of the prelate across the green turf of the links. He seemed to be borne on the wings of the wind, and each leap he took must have covered at least twenty yards. He gave me the impression of a grotesque competitor in an unearthly game of " Hop, skip, and leap." At length, after an elapse of perhaps fifteen seconds, I saw him halt in the distance about twenty yards from the red flag of the hole. Then he turned and faced us, as if patiently awaiting the next shot.   I little guessed what his purpose was.   His figure was clearly outlined against a distant crowd of some two or three hundred assembled behind the final hole to witness the end of this unprecedented struggle.

XVI

AN EXCITING FINISH

M Y ball was duly fished out of the burn and dropped behind my shoulder. I returned my own faithless driver to Kirkintulloch, and once again took hold of the Cardinal's. As I did so a telepathic throb of excitement passed through the bystanders.

I played the shot.

It eclipsed all my former efforts. I never have seen, nor shall I ever see again, such a hard-hit ball. With a trajectory scarcely higher than that of a rifle bullet at a medium range, it winged its way straight to the hole, dropping eventually within a yard or so of His Eminence. And then, straining my eyes, I saw a sight that startled me into a sudden realisation of the latter's purpose. He

had, so to speak, fielded the ball—that is
to say, he had dashed towards it as it fell ;
and now, by a series of nervous but skilful
kicks, he was directing its course straight
to the hole !   The red skirts were held high
in his hands, and the white bony legs
flashed to and fro as he sped in the wake
of the running globe.   I could not, of
course, actually see the ball, but, by an
intuition that admitted of no doubt whatever, I knew what he was up to.   I held
my breath in an agony of suspense as
nearer and nearer to the red flag flew the
gaunt figure of the Cardinal.   I swear my
heart stopped beating, and the paralysed
crowd seemed similarly affected, though
the sight that I saw was mercifully denied
to its eyes.   There was no doubt about it.
The Cardinal had so manipulated the ball
that I had holed out in three.

But the match was not yet over.

What Lindsay's feelings at the moment
were I know not, but he managed to play
a clever second stroke that landed him on
the green, some seven feet from the hole.

And now came the supreme moment.

If Lindsay holed his put we halved the match, if he failed I won the day.

Such was the pressure of the excited crowd that only the most strenuous efforts enabled the rope holders to maintain a clear circular space round the hole. It measured about fifteen yards in diameter, and within this charmed circle stood Lindsay and his caddie, Wetherby and Kirkintulloch, old Jock Johnson (the keeper of the green), Hanbury-Smith (the captain of the golf club), and myself. All other spectators were without the pale, with the important exception of the Cardinal.

I looked about me. My part in the game was over. I had but to watch and wait. I was thankful the final shot was Lindsay's and not mine.

The faces of my betting friends had changed again in expression, and become drawn and strained. The unfortunate gentlemen no longer chattered and chuckled. The magnet of luck was again slowly but surely attracting golden coins from the

" I SAW THE CARDINAL BLOW WITH MIGHT AND MAIN "

depths of their purses, and such pangs could only be borne with dumb fortitude.

The crowd were so terribly congested that two women fainted. I looked anxiously at Mrs. Gunter, but—thank Heaven!—the rich carmine still glowed on her cheeks.

At length, putter in hand, Lindsay approached his ball, and even the breathing of the crowd seemed to be suspended.

I moved to a spot some six feet from the hole, on the opposite side to Lindsay. As I did so my eyes fell on the ground, and I saw a startling and curious sight.

My terrible ally, the Cardinal, had stretched himself at full length, face downward, on the turf, so that his ghastly head was directly over the hole and his shadowy feet close to mine.

A sense of faintness crept over me.

As in a red mist I saw Lindsay strike the ball. I saw it travelling straight and sure to the hole!

And then—heavens above us!—I saw the Cardinal take a quick and gulping breath, and blow with might and main against the skilfully directed ball! It reached the edge of the hole, trembled a moment on the brink, and then ran off at an angle and lay still on the turf a couple of inches from the hole!

I had won the match.

A tumult sounded in my ears, the sky turned a blazing scarlet, the crowd swam before my eyes, and of a sudden I fell prone on the turf with my nose plunged in the fateful hole!

*   *   *   *   *

When I came to myself I found kind friends grouped about me, and my head resting luxuriously in Mrs. Gunter's lap. I think I should have been perfectly happy and content with this state of things, had I not unforunately just at that moment caught a glimpse of the ubiquitous Cardinal standing ridiculously on his head and kicking his heels in mid air in an ecstasy of frenzied glee.

The sight so upset me that I went off a second time into a dead faint.

XVII

AND LAST

AGAIN I was myself, and this time I felt revived and strong. I rose to my feet. Immediately the crowd closed round me and acclaimed me with cheers and yells. Presently I found myself being carried shoulder-high by a dozen lusty caddies, Kirkintulloch heading their progress with proud bearing and gleaming eye.

A thousand voices were howling " See, the conquering hero comes ! " A thousand hats and handkerchiefs were waving in the air. A thousand smiling faces beamed up into mine.

Mrs. Gunter cried out to me, as I passed her in triumphal procession, " You'll dine with the Lowchesters to-night, won't you ? "

And turning a smiling and radiant face to her, I answered, " I will."

I was the idol of the hour, not—I may add—an altogether new experience.

At length, after what seemed an eternity of acclamation and adulation, I was set down in the great bay window of the club, and immediately surrounded by all members who had *not* made bets with me. Fulsome flattery, genuine congratulation, and general admiration were showered on me. At writing-tables in distant corners of the room I saw my betting friends busily writing out cheques. They did not seem inclined to participate in the enthusiastic ovation. But what did I care?

Surfeited with the overwhelming tributes to my achievement (and, I fancy, to my personality), I broke away from my friends, only to be seized again by my escort of caddies and carried shoulder-high in the direction of the *Metropole*. The sturdy fellows finally deposited me on the top step of the main entrance to the hotel, and I stood facing the seething crowd.

Here a fresh outburst of applause greeted me from my fellow-guests and the domestic staff.

I bowed incessantly right and left.

" Speech ! Speech ! " now rang out on every side from a thousand throats, and I felt that if only to get rid of them, I must say something. So holding aloft my right hand as a token that I accepted the invitation, and in the profound silence instantly produced by my action, I said—

" My friends, I thank you. I have excelled in all other games, and why not in golf ? Again I thank you."

The simple words completely captivated them, and I retired indoors to a volley of tumultuous and long-continued cheers.

As an example of how trivial things often imprint themselves on our dazed memories during crises in our lives, I remember noting, as I passed through the hall to my suite of rooms, an immense pile of luggage, evidently just arrived, and labelled " The Prince Vladimir Demidoff." I had not heard of his intention to visit

St. Magnus. In fact, I don't think I'd ever heard of the man at all.

Reaching my room, I stretched myself on a couch, lit a cigarette, and got Wetherby to bring me a stiff brandy-and-soda. At last, thought I, I had breathing space. Imagine, then, my consternation and irritation when, on opening my eyes—I had closed them for a moment as I revelled in the first deep draught of my " peg "— I beheld, seated opposite me, His Eminence !

" Upon my soul ! " I cried, " this is too bad. You swore—— "

" Hud yer wheesht ! " interrupted the Cardinal. " I'm here to thank ye and bid ye ' gude-bye.' "

" I'm glad to hear it," I muttered, sulkily.

" Ye've focht a grand fecht," he proceeded, " an' I'm much obleegea tae ye. But, man, there's ae thing that worrits me extraordinar'. Ye ken, I had tae cheat ! I aye played fair in the auld days, and it gaed agin' the grain tae blaw on Lindsay's ba' at the last put, but what could I dae ?

Hooever, it canna be helpit. The queer thing is that noo that my revenge is complete, it doesna seem to gratify me muckle. Hech, sir!—life, moartal or speeritual's guy disappintin'. For a' that I'm much obleeged, an' ye'll never see me mair. Gude-bye!"

And with that he faded into space, and, truth to tell, he has honourably abstained from haunting me since.

Sheer physical fatigue precluded the possibility of anything in the nature of psychical research, or even of attempting to think out the weird supernatural experiences I had gone through.

I was dozing off into a gentle sleep when Wetherby opened the door and informed me that Kirkintulloch was waiting below, and would be proud if I could grant him a short interview.

I consented, and presently Kirkintulloch appeared.

" It's no' for the guinea I've come, sir," he began (I've no doubt, by way of a gentle reminder); " I thocht ye'd be glad o' a card wi' yer score, an' I've had it made oot."

He handed me a card, and on it I read the score :—

Out, 3 3 4 3 4 5 3 2 3 . 30
In, 3 2 3 4 5 3 3 4 3 . 30
                                    —
        Total . . . 60

" Ye're a credit to my teachin', sir," he continued, " an' I'm real prood o' ye. The record for thae links is seventy-twa, and ye're jist a clean dozen below that. The likes o' it was never seen. It's a fact. Ay ! an' long after a'body here's dead ye'll still hud the record. I little thocht I had pit ma ain style sae coampletely into ye ! Ye're a pairfect marvel ! "

" Thank you," I muttered wearily.

" I see ye're tired, sir, an' I'll no keep ye, but jist afore I gang, wad ye mind showin' me thae queer-like clubs ye played wi' ? "

" By all means," said I. " Wetherby, where are the clubs ? "

" Ain't you got 'em, sir ? " asked the latter, with some surprise.

" Not I ! " I answered. " You had them."

" Well, sir, I can't quite tell 'ow it is, but in the crowd I suddenly felt 'em slip out from under my arm, and look as I would I couldn't lay eyes on 'em after that. I supposed some friend of yours had taken them out of curiosity, and meant to bring 'em to you, sir."

" Dinna fash yersel'," broke in Kirkintulloch ; " if they're in St. Magnus I'll lay hands on them, never fear. Gude nicht, sir ! "

And so that admirable caddie passed out of my life. I tipped him well (and I've since been told he paid me the high- —if deplorable—compliment of a week's continuous intoxication), but from that day to this no mortal eye has seen the bewitched clubs of the ghostly Cardinal Archbishop of St. Magnus.

Much revived by two hours' sound and dreamless sleep, I dressed at half-past seven, and a few minutes before eight I started for the Lowchesters' house.

It had somehow got abroad that I was dining there, and a large crowd had assembled in front of the hotel. I was again received with an outburst of cheers, and subsequently escorted to my destination to a lustily sung chorus of " For he's a jolly good fellow ! "

Arrived at the Lowchesters' gates, I bade the kindly crowd good night, and retired from their sight to a final volley of echoing cheers.

I need not describe the welcome I received from my host and hostess, Mrs. Gunter, and the other guests. Even Lindsay spoke to me tactfully on the subject of our match, expressing genuine admiration of my performance, though I was slightly startled when he said, " In fact, I consider your play to-day nothing short of supernatural."

So did I, but I didn't venture to say so.

The dinner was delightful. Excellent

food, perfect wine, charming people, and myself the centre of interest. I ask no more at such a function.

I took my hostess in to dinner of course but on my other side was Mrs. Gunter, exquisitely dressed in a Parisian triumph of eau-de-Nil velvet with groups of mauve and purple pansies. Her wonderful complexion was more ravishing than ever in the soft lamplight. Indeed it seemed to have specially adapted itself to the requirements of her delicately tinted gown. Her hands and arms had the bloom of peaches, and her luxuriant hair, dark underneath, was a mist of everchanging gold on the top.

Several times during dinner I saw the jet-black lashes raised, and felt her glorious eyes regarding me with the rapt gaze of hero-worship.

Well, to-night I should know, for weal or woe, what fortune the Fates held in store for me.

When the ladies had left us I drew Lindsay aside on the pretence of examining some engravings in the hall, and as soon as we were alone I touched on the subject uppermost in my mind.

"I think it only right to tell you, my dear Lindsay," I began, "that to-night I shall propose to Mrs. Gunter, and if by any chance she should dismiss me, then I leave the field clear for you. I have to thank you for all the courtesy you have shown during my visit to St. Magnus, and I sincerely trust that whatever may happen we shall always remain friends."

"As far as I'm concerned you may be sure of that," replied Lindsay. "But it does seem to me that you've been labouring under a delusion. I've never desired to propose to Mrs. Gunter. And even if I wanted to, I couldn't. I'm a married man, with three of a family. More than that, I'm very deeply in love with my wife, and not at all with Mrs. Gunter."

"But—good heavens!" I exclaimed, "surely we agreed——"

"If you remember," he interrupted, "that night in the Racing Club, I wanted to explain these things, **and** you simply wouldn't hear me."

" Then," I continued blankly, as in a sudden flash of memory I recalled the fact he alluded to, " we've been fighting for nothing ? "

" Exactly," he replied.

In silence we shook hands, and the matter dropped.

Presently we joined the ladies in the drawing-room, and after a decent interval I drew Mrs. Gunter aside. We sat by each other on a couch concealed from view by a group of palms. A pretty girl in white was playing the " Moonlight Sonata."

I admit it at once—my heart was beating. I wished I had rehearsed the rôle I was about to play. Then I reflected that I had often witnessed proposals on the stage, so taking a leaf from that reliable book I cleared my throat.

" Mrs. Gunter," I began, " may I say Katherine ? "

" Ah ! So it has come to this ! " she

murmured, lowering her eyes with the most captivating grace.

"Yes, this," I whispered passionately. "This, that I love you and only you! This, that I am here to ask you to be my wife!"

"It can never be!" she murmured conventionally, and a low cry, half sob, half sigh, escaped her.

"Katherine!" I cried, "why not?"

"Because," she answered slowly, and as if the words were dragged from her, "I have lost every penny of my fortune. And a penniless woman I cannot, will not come to you. Unless——" and her voice trembled into silence.

She was wearing several thousand pounds' worth of diamonds at the time, but somehow I didn't grasp the sparkling contradiction.

Now I am a man of quick resolution. I can grasp a situation in a moment. In a flash I realised that I alone could never afford to keep this beautiful creature in surroundings worthy of her, at least not without such personal sacrifice as at my time of life would be extremely inconvenient. I am but a younger son. To force her then to marry me under such circumstances would be a cruelty to her and an injustice to myself.

Afraid, therefore, that the murmured word " Unless—— " was about to open up possibilities not altogether desirable, I broke the silence with—

" And so you dismiss me ? "

She looked at me for a moment in blank surprise.

Then the ghost of a faint smile flickered over her face, as she answered—

" Yes, *so I dismiss you !* "

I gave a suitable sigh.

The " Moonlight Sonata " was over, and poor Katherine rose.

I followed her to a group of guests in the centre of the room, and as I did so she turned and said—

" I was going to say, ' *Unless* you can induce my future husband to give me up,' when you interrupted me."

" Your future husband ! " I exclaimed aghast.

" Yes," she answered serenely ; " let me introduce you to him."

And touching the sleeve of the good-looking foreigner who had taken her in to dinner, she said—

" Vladimir, let me present Major Gore," adding to me, " Prince Vladimir Demidoff. Didn't you know that we are to be married next week ? "

I murmured confused words of congratulation, and escaped to Lady Lowchester's side.

" Are they really going to be married ? " I asked her.

" Of course they are ! " replied my hostess. " Why shouldn't they ? "

" But—but," I stammered, " she's lost every penny of her fortune ! "

' Not she ! " replied Lady Lowchester, with a merry ringing laugh. " That's what she tells every man who proposes to her. She says she finds it an excellent gauge of devotion."

" I see," I answered.

I stood still for a moment. Then I walked over to Lowchester and asked him which was the best morning train from St. Magnus to London.

*   *   *   *   *

I did not feel justified in keeping for my own use the £10,000 I had won, but it may interest the reader to know that with it I founded the now flourishing and largely patronised " Home for Inebriate Caddies."

THE END